Dominique Moyse Steinberg, DSW

The Social Work Student's Research Handbook

Pre-publication
REVIEWS,
COMMENTARIES,
EVALUATIONS . . .

"This handbook is designed to complement textbooks and research courses, and to be used as a refresher whenever research is being considered or discussed. Readers will quickly find reference to their day-to-day queries about research in this text that encourages reluctant researchers to believe they can and want to research. The content is laid out logically, with brief explanations and encouraging asides along with summaries of the main points and short exercises to reinforce learning and build confidence. As a social work educator, I will certainly find a place for this handy guide in my library."

Pauline Noden, MSc
Head of Department for Social
Work Studies,
Buckinghamshire Chilterns
University College,
High Wycombe, England

"Steinberg has done an excellent job in writing a supplemental handbook for students and others involved in social work research. This handbook will be invaluable for quick reference while designing and reviewing research projects. This book will be a useful tool for students and practitioners who may be occasional, or 'rusty,' researchers. Steinberg's text will be continually referenced as students operationalize their research projects, practitioners design evaluative studies, and grant writers develop proposals. Students can use the handbook to clarify the more involved discussions of design and statistics contained in many texts."

Gary Lounsberry, PhD
Associate Professor,
Division of Social Work,
Florida Gulf Coast University

More pre-publication
REVIEWS, COMMENTARIES, EVALUATIONS . . .

"The publication of this handbook is a gift to both social work students and their instructors. The book is clear, comprehensive, and well written, and will appeal to students coping with 'research anxiety' and to instructors trying to de-escalate that anxiety. Dr. Steinberg demonstrates that research is not a solitary, number-crunching activity. She demystifies the practice of research and encourages students to see research as a collaborative, curiousity-driven process.

The book moves logically in a simple but not simplistic fashion that engages the readers' attention and conveys all of the necessary information. It addresses issues up front and with engaging clarity using relevant, practical examples. Dr. Steinberg walks students through a process of critical thinking to become more confident researchers. Using this book, students will have a better idea about what they want to learn, what assumptions they are making, how to clarify their thinking, and what methods are best suited to their research work."

Margaret M. Wright, PhD
Assistant Professor,
School of Social Work and Family Studies,
University of British Columbia

The Haworth Social Work Practice Press
An Imprint of The Haworth Press, Inc.
New York • London • Oxford

The Social Work Student's Research Handbook

THE HAWORTH SOCIAL WORK PRACTICE PRESS
Social Work Practice in Action
Marvin D. Feit
Editor in Chief

Human Behavior in the Social Environment: Interweaving the Inner and Outer World by Esther Urdang

Family Health Social Work Practice: A Knowledge and Skills Casebook edited by Francis K. O. Yuen, Gregory J. Skibinski, and John T. Pardeck

African-American Social Workers and Social Policy edited by Tricia B. Bent-Goodley

The Social Work Student's Research Handbook by Dominique Moyse Steinberg

Mental Health Practice for Children and Youth: A Strengths and Well-Being Model by Lonnie R. Helton and Mieko Kotake Smith

The Social Work Student's Research Handbook

Dominique Moyse Steinberg, DSW, CSW, ACSW

The Haworth Social Work Practice Press
An Imprint of The Haworth Press, Inc.
New York • London • Oxford

Published by

The Haworth Social Work Practice Press, an imprint of The Haworth Press, Inc., Alice Street, Binghamton, NY 13904-1580.

Cover design by Marylouise E. Doyle.

Library of Congress Cataloging-in-Publication Data

Steinberg, Dominique Moyse.
    The social work student's research handbook / Dominique Moyse Steinberg.
        p. cm.
Includes bibliographical references and index.
    ISBN 0-7890-1480-7 (case : alk. paper)—ISBN 0-7890-1481-5 (soft : alk. paper)
    1. Social service—Research—Handbooks, manuals, etc. 2. Social work education. I. Title.
    HV11.S77 2004
    362.3'072—dc22
                                                                                                    2003016144

This book is dedicated to
Rebecca Donovan, in memoriam,
a research teacher who encouraged me to laugh
when I wanted to cry in research class

and to
Roselle Kurland,
who eventually taught me to teach the subject.

ABOUT THE AUTHOR

Dominique Moyse Steinberg, DSW, is founder of The Center for the Advancement of Mutual Aid, based in Vermont and New York. She has been a faculty member at the Hunter College School of Social Work where she served as field advisor to MSW and BSW students, supervised social work interns, and offered private research and writing tutorials to doctoral students. Dr. Steinberg has provided services to various organizations, including the New York Family Reception Center (policy/practice); the Child Welfare League of America and the New York Academy for Educational Development (program design); the Children's Defense Fund, Manhattan Teen Pregnancy Network, and the Parsons-Sage Institute (program design/practice); Bronx-Lebanon Hospital and the New York Sisters of the Good Shepherd (practice).

Dr. Steinberg is an editorial board member of *Social Work with Groups;* a Fellow of the Academy of Certified Social Workers; a member, former board member, and former Chair of Endowment for the Association for the Advancement of Social Work with Groups; a member of the NYC/New England chapters of NASW; and a former consultant to the NASW Committee on Inquiry. After teaching at New York University and Hunter College School of Social Work for several years, Dr. Steinberg now commutes between New York City and New England, where she teaches group work practice, research, and writing for publication at Smith College School of Social Work in Northampton, Massachusetts.

CONTENTS

Preface

Social work research courses are mandated by the Council on Social Work Education. Engaging in scientific inquiry is mandated by the National Association of Social Workers Code of Ethics. From all corners of the profession are calls for "evidence-based" practice. However, after years of professional practice, teaching, and conversing with colleagues, I know that most people who enter social work do not describe themselves as "scientifically minded" and are frightened, even phobic, of research. In fact, in my experience it is more common to hear students say that they have chosen social work as a career because of its humanistic, experiential, and interactive dimensions rather than because of any aptitude for or desire to conduct scientific inquiry. *I didn't enter social work to engage in math or science!* I hear many students say. *I entered it to help people!* Thus, over years of teaching hundreds of social work students I have encountered a common thread of resistance to learning (and even thinking) about research.

As a teacher I've also had opportunities to use various textbooks. They all cover an enormous amount of material of which both intellectual and practical sense must be made, and although it's appropriate for them to be comprehensive, that very attempt to "cover it all" has prompted this small and, I hope, user-friendly handbook.

Clearly, integration of content should occur through classroom process, but I hear complaints such as the following over and over again: *The first chapter is okay, but then I get lost in all the technical stuff.* Or *The beginning on theory and philosophical underpinnings of research is so abstruse!* Or *I'm discouraged and even more anxious than before I started to read.* Or *I'm just so nervous about research that I'm afraid even to read about it!* I have heard some students say that they underline every sentence as they read because it is so difficult to extrapolate the supposedly essential material from the surrounding discussion!

My hope, therefore, is that this handbook will enhance the user's ability to pick out the essence of social research methods, regardless of the primary textbook used, that it will help the student make better use of the classroom as a resource, that it will facilitate the integration of research into other professional study (such as practice account-ability, field work, organizational research projects, etc.) and prac-tice, and that it will help whoever uses it to become a better learner, producer, and consumer of social work research and, as such, a better social worker.

Introduction

The purpose of this handbook is to help you take and keep hold of the major concepts, principles, and steps of the research process using social work as context. Many, many research books are on the shelves today, most of them hundreds of pages and thousands of words. Many of them are very good. They speak to all of the issues, from thinking about what to study (problem formulation) and why it should be studied (professional significance) to different ways of inquiring (design and methodology) to discussing what you found (analysis and dissemination of results). Usually included throughout those discussions is special attention to ethics, both conceptually and methodologically. In other words, lots of material is covered in one place, and it can be difficult to pick out from all the narrative, details, and examples those points that either *must be kept in mind or need to be understood in order to move from one methodological step to the next.*

This handbook, therefore, is intended to complement, not replace, those books. It's for reading after them or with them or even perhaps before them—for using on your own time as a refresher, say, after reading about problem formulation in order to help you cull the "nuts and bolts" of formulating your own problem for study. It is for consultation while you are in the library or on the bus. It is to reference as someone speaks of correlational design or inferential stats and you find yourself saying, *Huh?* It's for using in the privacy and quiet of your thinking, outside of the classroom—for keeping the "operatic highlights" of the research process in mind as you move through what is admittedly both complex and simple (though not simplistic).

Social work research books say pretty much the same thing. Authors have various points of view, of course, and personal ways of presenting the material, of trying to help you make sense of what they're saying. Regardless, major points are always and unavoidably surrounded by thousands upon thousands of other words so that the heart of the matter is easily lost, subsumed by long theoretical narratives accompanied by example after example.

In a nutshell, then, the purpose of this handbook is to help you wade through all of that, to help you pick out what's really important—the crux of each issue. How so? First, it will help you feel better and more confident about engaging in research. For example, are there moments in formulating a problem when you think your understanding should be getting clearer but you're getting more confused instead? As Chapter 1 says, that's okay. It happens to everyone. It's part and parcel of problem formulation; this handbook lets you know it's normal and what to do next to become less overwhelmed. Second, it will help you clarify basic or central concepts and principles in each step of the method—what you *must* consider at each decision-making point. Third, it will help you connect those steps to one another, both conceptually and practically. Fourth, it will help you integrate theory (what should be done) with the real world (what's feasible).

This book does not engage in a discussion of ethical obligations and implications of research. Occasional references to ethics and etiquette are made throughout the book, but for a full and meaningful understanding of ethics in general and, more specifically, of human subjects review protocols and informed consent procedures, refer to the many textbooks on the subject, your course work, instructors, and colleagues, and the National Association of Social Workers *Code of Ethics* manual. This manual is available through any NASW office or social work school and outlines very specifically what research should do, may do, and cannot do and why in each case.

The twenty-two chapters of this book are organized as follows: Chapter 1 discusses *problem formulation,* the first and perhaps most challenging, artistic but fun part of research, when you have an opportunity to play around with and decide which of all possible questions you'd like to ask. Chapter 2, devoted to *reviewing the literature,* will help you understand why and how to read and think about what others have said and done in your topic of interest. Chapter 3 describes the role of and discusses similarities and differences between *hypotheses and research questions.* Chapter 4 talks about variables—how to conceptualize, define, and measure them. Chapter 5 explains the role of *assumptions.* Chapter 6, *design options,* provides an overview of each of four research design types and clarifies the connection between a study's purpose and selecting design. Chapters 7 through 10 describe in greater detail *exploratory, descriptive, experimental,* and *correlational* and *quasi-experimental* designs, respectively. Chapter 11 explains the role of *plausible alternative explanations* in certain design types. Chapter 12 presents the major concepts and principles of *practice evaluation,* along with examples of a few basic designs. Chapter 13 presents an overview of *program evaluation.* Chapter 14 describes the role and meaning of *reliability* and *validity* in instrument design. Chapter 15 outlines and discusses the methods and implications of the various *sampling strategies.* Major advantages, disadvantages, and issues to consider of three major *data collection methods* are presented in Chapter 16. Chapter 17 offers an overview of *data analysis.* Chapter 18 outlines the major concepts, principles, and issues to consider in *qualitative analysis.* Both focusing on quantitative data analysis, Chapters 19 and 20 describe *descriptive* and *inferential statistics,* respectively. Chapter 21 presents an overview of a few common *statistical tests.* Finally, Chapter 22 wraps up the book with an endnote.

Examples are used as often as possible to illustrate major points. Each chapter ends with a list of *major points to remember* and one or more *self-test exercises* intended to help you make immediate and personal use of the chapter's content.

Chapter 1

Problem Formulation: What to Study

(Getting Started)

KEY CONCEPTS

back-and-forth thinking
felt difficulties
focus
inquiry
internal versus external motivation
pleading a cause
problem
problem formulation
problem identification
professional significance

SELECTING A STUDY TOPIC

Moving Through the Funnel

If it is time to select a study topic and you are interested in many areas, then it's time to begin *problem identification,* part one of problem formulation. Part two of the process takes the same title as the whole process, *problem formulation.* Problem identification is a search for a general area of interest that has professional meaning. Problem formulation is the articulation of a research problem in statement form.

So, What's a Research Problem?

In research lingo the term *problem* has no negative connotation. We could just as well use *issue, concern, dilemma,* and *question* or even *gap in knowledge* that needs exploration, examination, or resolution.

Let's say you're invited to two holiday dinners at the same time. You have a problem, but it's a wonderful problem! So don't begin this process with a negative mind-set. Your research problem is simply the specific topic that you choose to study.

Mind-Set

Think of problem formulation as a funnel through which your thinking must pass (see Figure 1.1). You can see that there's a lot more space at the top than the bottom, right? That's because you begin this process by considering ideas, by brainstorming, by examining many different possible areas to explore, study, and learn about.

Begin with a good long stretch of sitting at the top rim as you ponder a broad area of interest to you *(problem identification),* maybe taking one step downward and then heading back up as new ideas and possibilities occur through reading, thinking, and talking with others. Then, as your thinking becomes increasingly refined, you continue down to the narrowest part of the funnel, each step representing further conceptual focus until you can articulate the problem (as hypothesis or question) clearly and specifically enough to pass completely through the neck.

As you do this, you may discover that there's more information on your topic than you realized and that it answers some or even many of your questions. You may find that new questions develop, making you more, rather than less, confused about what to study. Don't get upset! Remember how to eat an elephant? One bite at a time. Attack a problem one piece at a time. Here your mantra is *read, think, talk, rest, read, think, talk, rest.* Things will come together.

It's okay if your thinking goes back and forth; bit by bit the process advancing. Every bit of thinking and rethinking brings you closer to clarity and focus. As you travel this particular funnel you may defy gravity by occasionally jumping back up a step or two to regroup, to change your interest or perspective ever so slightly before starting

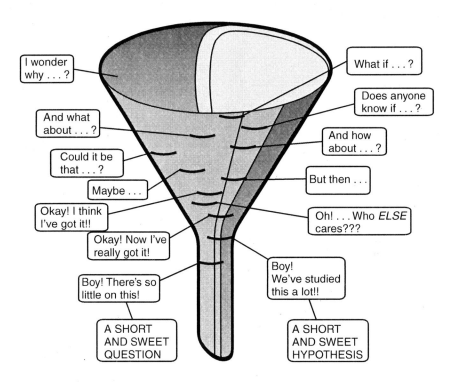

FIGURE 1.1. Problem Formulation Funnel

back down again. Back and forth thinking is a norm, not a failure of good decision making. Much of problem formulation is playing around with ideas, with revisitation and revision part of the journey.

You're Not Secretly Trying to Plead a Cause, Right?

Sometimes people get stuck in this process because they already have ideas that they really want to get across to others—to write a position paper, to promote a treasured belief. That mind-set, however, makes it absolutely impossible for you to remain in a questioning mode—which is what you're supposed to do right now. So remember, this part of research is *all* and *only* about developing a question, *not* how to get an answer (your values, beliefs, attitudes, assumptions, or desires) across to others. *The guiding principle here is to formulate a study that actually studies!*

Can You Live with Any Result?

Whatever question you end up with, you need to think about the acceptability of potential results. Will it be all right with you if results suggest something other than what you thought they would? That your approach to practice is less effective than you hoped? What if results are contrary to your values or expectations—surprising in some way? Maybe your findings are not all that pleasant to your ego, for example. If you can accept these possibilities, then go ahead and study that topic, ask that question, test that hypothesis. Be honest with yourself. If you can imagine that some findings would be difficult for you to live with, find another topic.

Who Cares About This Study Besides You?

Now you're worried that your questions are interesting only to you and not as brilliant as, say, those of Albert Einstein—or even those of your peers? Don't worry! In fact, research is rarely cosmic in scope, and the point here isn't to create an *éclat*. Don't get caught up in *bigger is better*. The point is to gain a piece of knowledge that will be of real and practical use. Maybe that's knowing more about how veteran practitioners incorporate certain cognitive tasks into their practice with addiction; maybe it's a closer look at a group treatment program; maybe it's an updated description of agency cases; maybe it's an exploration of current difficulties in a refugee camp; and on and on ad infinitum. If you can argue for the utility of prospective findings to social work, then you have a legitimate pursuit.

Motivation: Internal versus External

On the other hand, not every form of inquiry is research. Some is therapy. Although we often develop professional interest in areas that hit close to home, here's the rub for research. If our motivation is strictly internal (self-study), then we're bound to engage in therapy rather than research. How does that look? You'll have difficulty designing an instrument (e.g., an interview guide) with professional distance. You'll lose any semblance of professional interest in the project as soon as your question is answered on your personal behalf. Your biases will weigh heavily upon your data analysis. Finally, you may simply become stuck, unable to complete the process because the content (literature, data collected, results, etc.) is too personally overwhelming.

NOW WHAT?

Now you work toward *balance*—between developing a problem that's of interest only to you and one that's too cosmic and unrealistic to pursue. How? *Don't go at it alone!* Talk to friends, teachers, colleagues—anyone who's interested and will listen. Problem formulation is rarely, if ever, carried out alone. The image of a lonely white coat tucked away in a lab, testing a theory no one else knows about doesn't pertain to social science research. Rather, for brainstorming and all such processes, the rule of thumb is *the more the merrier!* One of the best ways to know if you're clear in your thinking and on target is when others in the know tell you so.

A lot to think about? Of course! That's what makes this the most difficult part of the process, but playing around with possibilities can also be much fun.

Ask Yourself

1. What do I want to know? What are some professional issues of interest to me, unanswered questions, gaps in my knowledge? You might begin by deciding if you're interested primarily in practice (conceptual approach, method, model, impact of national policies, etc.), population (practitioners, women, children, homeless persons, nursing home residents, people hospitalized for a certain illness, etc.), or problem (issues of education, addiction, teen pregnancy, attachment, resilience, mental illness, etc.).
2. Now get more specific within the context of your response to number 1. What particular issues am I interested in? Social work practice in medical settings? Nature of professional education? Statistics on homelessness? Issues that confront home-

less persons who seek work? Alcoholism among the elderly? Grief work in treatment with addicted persons? History of workfare legislation? Impact of current legislation on single-parent households? Day treatment programs for mentally retarded persons? Treatment approaches for working with abused adolescents?

3. Now, what difference would the study of this issue make? Who else would be interested in such a study? Remember, even with personal interest, your question must be of professional utility. If you can identify concrete ways in which the results could be used by other professionals, you're on your way.

4. Finally, would any possible results of this study be acceptable to me? Yes? Great. Not sure? Do more thinking. Be honest; you'll save yourself lots of angst later.

MAJOR POINTS TO REMEMBER

- Social work research mandates implications for practice, recommendations for helping us do what we do better.
- Problem formulation has two steps. *Identification* refers to your broad topic area; *formulation* refers to the angle from which you're going to examine that area.
- At the end of this process you will have developed a research problem simply stated in either a hypothesis or question form that you can repeat over and over from memory.
- Don't assign a negative connotation to the term *research problem.* A research problem simply represents some gap in knowledge that needs closing through study.
- Think of problem formulation as descending a funnel starting with a long stretch on top as you identify a broad area of interest. Moving down through its neck, each step represents further conceptual refinement.
- A research problem is *not* how to tell others an answer you already have; it's your idea of a felt difficulty, some gap in our professional knowledge, that needs answering.
- All potential results of a research study must be acceptable, whether they confirm, disconfirm, surprise, or disappoint.

- Research is rarely cosmic in scope; the point is to gain a piece of knowledge that will be of real and practical use.
- Not every form of inquiry is research. Some is therapy. In research, the felt difficulty to be examined is external; in therapy, the felt difficulty to be examined is internal.

EXERCISE

Test Yourself

Repeat your research problem (that hypothesis or question) five times without looking at the paper on which it's written. Can you do it? *Remember:* the more simply stated, the more likely you will stay on track.

Chapter 2

Using the Literature

(Who Has Said What About This Already? So What?)

KEY CONCEPTS

accountability
context
critiquing
discussion
focus
heartbeat
organization
reading around
related literature
relatedness
reporting
reviewing

INTRODUCTION

There is a logical relationship between what's already known about your topic (as reflected by the literature) and the way you ultimately formulate your research problem. You can't know the nature of that relationship, however, until you've reviewed that literature. Your understanding of this relationship begins with a search for all of the work, conceptual and empirical, that pertains to your area of interest. It culminates in a written review that presents, discusses, analyzes, and critiques that work and connects it to the rationale for your own work.

PART 1: THE SEARCH

Mind-Set

The mind-set for the search is one of trying to make yourself "intelligent." Once you select a general topic and read what others have said or done about it, you gain the knowledge and insight to formulate a problem intelligently. Then, by reviewing that literature in written form, you provide both a foundation and context for your own work and make your consumers intelligent as well. Only when they understand how your work fits into the overall picture, both historically and contemporaneously, can they assess the meaning and impact of your results.

Reading Around

A lot to think about? Absolutely! And the way to begin is by "reading around." Start with social work literature, because your study is in, of, and for the benefit of that field. Then move to other bodies of literature that may speak to your topic, such as psychology, education—even medicine, religion, philosophy, politics, economics, and probably others. You might look in popular literature, too, such as newspapers and magazines. Ultimately, you may find that more than one body of literature speaks to your subject.

Remember, the goal is to read enough to be able to articulate your research problem in a sentence that truly reflects what you want to know and is simple enough to repeat over and over without looking at it in writing! Maybe it will have a period after it, in which case you'll work from now on to test a *hypothesis*. Or maybe it will end with a question mark, in which case you'll work to answer a *question*. (Hypotheses and questions are discussed further in Chapter 3.)

Going About It the Right Way

What goes into a good search? Start by seeking the most current material (usually in professional journals) and work backward. Be sure to search their bibliographies for leads. Then move to books, encyclopedias, and, for contemporary events, newspaper indexes. Don't overlook *Bibliographic Index, Bibliography of Bibliographies,* and similar standard reference sources. Some catalogs are useful to locate books as well, such as the *Cumulative Book Index* and *Books in Print.* Library of Congress services such as Medlars, ERIC, and University Microfilms may also be useful. Of course, search the Web for literature from professional and popular databases, public libraries, and public and private organizations and associations.

When Is It Enough?

You've done enough research when you find that wherever you look you run into titles of books and articles you've read already—in other words, when you've pretty much exhausted the literature on your topic. Of course, "the literature" is not static; articles are being published all the time. In real-world terms, then, "enough" is when you think you know enough about the subject to state a clear and focused problem for study, design a reliable and valid instrument, and develop a sound data-collection plan. Might there be yet a piece of literature you've *not* read as you implement your study? Sure. There's always more to read, but that's okay. If you have a chance to read and integrate a new piece of literature later, fine. If not, it will go into the next study, be it yours or someone else's.

Tools of the Trade

Valuable references are often encountered unexpectedly, so be prepared. First, carry index cards to jot down title, author, publisher, date of publication, and relevant pages, such as journal or chapter pages. Also note how that particular piece of literature relates to your problem, how and where you might use it in your review, and any commentary that seems important. Be sure to critique and not just describe what the literature says. In the alternative, use a small memo machine, into which you can speak your entry and transcribe from later. Always keep in mind your hypothesis or question as you read, reminding yourself how, exactly, each piece of literature fits into what you're doing. Make that relationship explicit in your notes. This will help prevent you from collecting a huge but haphazard and useless bibliography. In fact, carry it around with you.

Keep a selection of brown market bags, hidden away somewhere but accessible and titled according to the themes that emerge from your literature review, ready to receive cut-out or copied sections of articles or certain quotes that pertain to those themes. You might also tape specific pieces of literature to a notebook with titled pages or even develop special folders in your computer system, but moving around the pieces of literature, which you are very likely to do when it comes time for final organization of your review, is easier to do from bag to bag than untaping and retaping. Also, it is often easier to develop a coherent pattern for the material when you can actually lay out pieces of paper and move them around from one theme to another, for example. Although you may well have several computer files for your literature, you might still want to have hard copies of both your own writing and that of others in order to play around, if you will, with the material. Pieces of literature often fit into more than one developing theme, and a well-developed literature review requires extensive organizing and reorganizing.

PART 2: WRITING THE REVIEW

Mind-Set

Think of this section as a discussion with a friend about what others have said and found on your subject. Just as you would offer commentary in that discussion, give the reader a sense of your own heartbeat in the review, i.e., what *you* think about what has been said and done.

Have a Plan

Begin with a tentative outline of major points to see if they make sense, and to determine how best to organize their order. Also, check for holes (what needs to be beefed up), redundancy (what can be tightened), and consider combining sections. Then use that outline to create as many headings and subheadings as needed to keep the conceptual flow clear, both for you and the reader. It's better to use too many headings than to make readers wade through long sections with no guidance. Remember, your purpose is to set the stage for your own study, to present your rationale and context for the work you have (in a proposal) or had (in a report) in mind.

Writing

Think in terms of an hourglass for each section and subsection. Begin from a comprehensive view with broad introductory statements; move to specifics with details (explanations, clarification, expansion, etc.) and examples; close with a broad summary statement and a conceptual transition to the next section.

Begin with classic literature, the earliest or most well-known thinking, writing, and research that has paved the way for your own work. These are efforts of "trailblazers" and provide a historic context, a conceptual lineage to current thinking. Then move to contemporaneous efforts to understand your topic.

Emphasize Relatedness

Keep your reader constantly aware of how the literature relates to your own study. Point out this relationship precisely and constantly. Don't be afraid of repetition. Remember that the reader doesn't have the same material in his or her head.

Be Accountable

Account for each study you cite by specifically stating its relationship to your research problem. Don't leave your readers hanging, wondering why you're talking about it. Make the connections clear. Unless you can establish such accountability, you'd do well to not use literature at all. Remember to properly cite literature to which you refer, including page references for direct quotes.

Integrate Your Heartbeat (What You Think)

Finally, don't write a chain of pointless isolated summaries of other people's writing or thinking, such as, "Jones says . . . Green says," etc. That is *not* a review; it's a report. The difference? A review is your heartbeat—what you think about what others have said and done. In other words, it demonstrates the relatedness of the literature to your research problem. A report is simply a description without analysis or critique.

MAJOR POINTS TO REMEMBER

- Searching the literature on your topic helps to develop an "intelligent" research problem.
- A good search begins by "reading around" in the body of literature most pertinent to your topic and then expanding to other possibly related literature, both professional and popular.
- The goal of a search is to read enough to be able to clearly articulate your research problem as a question or hypothesis.
- A search begins with current material and works backward. It includes articles, books, encyclopedias, catalogs, bibliographies, Web-based material, and even popular literature.
- "Enough" is when you frequently find titles of books and articles you've read already.
- Always carry index cards to jot down unexpected references.
- Think of the written review of the literature as a discussion with a friend about what others have said and found on your subject.
- Throughout, however, remember to give credit where credit is due through proper references and citations.
- Use an outline to organize your review; create headings and subheadings to keep the conceptual flow of your discussion clear.

- Begin discussions from a comprehensive perspective, move to specifics, and close with broad summary and transitional statements.
- Keep your reader aware of how each piece of literature relates to your study.
- Don't write a chain of pointless isolated summaries of other people's writing or thinking.

EXERCISES

Self-Assessment Number 1

As you read around, ask yourself these questions with regard to your topic area:

1. How does my *thinking* fit into the general picture, both historically and contemporaneously?
2. How does my *formulation* compare to those of previous studies on this topic?
3. Does the literature suggest a consensus of thought on my topic, or are there some important controversies, debates, or divergences? If so, what kind of contribution would my study make?

Self-Assessment Number 2

1. Free write what you think you know about your topic. Don't pay too much attention to form and grammar, etc. Instead, focus on the substance.
2. Read what you've written and pick out major themes. What is the history of your topic? How did social work come to pay attention to it? Has it even done so? Perhaps other fields have explored it more than social work. If so, say so, and discuss the topic from those perspectives. Who are important figures—scholars, researchers, advocates, etc.? How have they contributed to our current understanding? What's happening today? The thinking? The research? What's missing, in your opinion? What's your understanding of the current gap in knowledge?

Answering these questions will help you develop a formal outline that expands what you've already written and, in that expansion, help you to make a case for your study.

I want to extend my special thanks to Dr. Roselle Kurland for sharing with me her literature review notes and handouts so many years ago.

Chapter 3

Working from Questions or Hypotheses

(To Ask or to Test? *That* Is the Question)

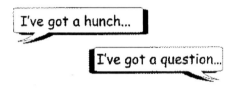

KEY CONCEPTS

conjecture
hypothesis
null hypothesis
proof
question
refutation
substantiation

INTRODUCTION

Should you work from a question or develop a hypothesis? Don't try to decide before gaining further clarity; there's a logical relationship between existing knowledge on your topic (which you learned by reviewing the literature) and how you finally formulate your research problem. "Reading around" clarifies your purpose, which then suggests a design and makes the choice relatively self-evident.

HYPOTHESES AND QUESTIONS

Basic Differences

Here's the essential difference between the two: a question asks and can receive a definitive answer; a hypothesis, however, can only be substantiated or refuted, never "proven." It is an educated guess—a hunch—that conjectures and then is tested for credibility. Note that the guess is *educated,* meaning that it's not just some off-the-wall proposition but one that is rooted in knowledge. This means that enough has been studied and written for there to be a body of knowledge in the first place.

So if little is known about your topic (or much is known but not from your particular angle of interest), chances are it will make good sense to formulate your problem as a question. On the other hand, if a great deal is known—enough to formulate an educated hunch about some relationship between variables—then a hypothesis may be in order.

Commonalities

Hypotheses and questions both serve as a framework—your guide for what you'll look at and how you'll look at it. Your hypothesis or question will be your concrete reference point for all future action (e.g., *What is it I want to know, again?* or *What should I do now?* or *Why should I do that?* or *Why am I reading this article?*) and your standard for analysis (e.g., *What am I looking for here, again?* and *What does it all mean?*). Whichever you end up with is what you stick to your forehead (figuratively, anyway) as a reminder of why you're doing whatever you're doing.

THE NOTION OF PROOF

While you're pondering this, remember that we never prove anything in social science; there is just too much fluidity in our subjects of interest. Of course, as noted previously, questions might be answered definitely, but hypotheses are only substantiated or refuted. So, even if it makes sense to articulate your problem as a hypothesis, forget your preconceived notions about proof! Instead, think *credible substantiation*—particularly within the study's context—and keep your implications for other contexts humble (i.e., conservative).

NULL HYPOTHESIS

If you do work from a hypothesis, you'll challenge it with one of several possible tests of statistical significance (see Chapters 20 and 21). This will, in effect, test the *null* version of your hypothesis. What in the world is that? Here are a few examples:

If your hypothesis is: Alcoholism and homelessness are related,
your null hypothesis is: No siree, they are *not* related.*

If your hypothesis is: Smoking causes lung cancer,
your null hypothesis is: No siree, smoking does *not* cause lung cancer.

If your hypothesis is: Race influences social workers' attitudes toward their clients,
your null hypothesis is: No siree, race does *not* influence their attitudes toward their clients.

If your hypothesis is: This ten-week special program will change teenagers' behavior,
your null hypothesis is: No siree, it will *not* change their behavior.

Note that a null hypothesis is *not* an opposite version of your original one; it simply nullifies your proposition, whatever it is.

Why, oh why, jump through such a hoop? Inherent in the formation of every null hypothesis is the following challenge to the researcher by our nemesis, Mr. Probability Theory, who says: *Guess what? Any differences or associations you find when you test this hypothesis are really due to chance or sampling error; so don't get too excited!*

Why such convolution? Simple, really. It's so easy to substantiate a beloved hypothesis (yes, even using stats or so-called hard numbers to do so) that scientific protocol methodology requires that you to do all you can to refute it (by trying to substantiate its *null* version). Then, if your original version still "holds water," your credibility is that much stronger. *After all,* you can say, *I did everything I could to*

---

*Of course, the "no sirees" are not a formal part of a null hypothesis! They're just here to make a point.

refute my own proposition, and guess what? It's still a good one! This is just another way of trying to keep research honest, and it's not such a bad idea.

IS QUESTION-DRIVEN RESEARCH
REAL RESEARCH?

Some people claim that the only "real" research is hypothesis-driven research and that question-driven studies are only precursors to the real thing. That's not true; especially not in social science research, which still has much to learn. Each type of study has value and makes sense under certain circumstances; neither one is subservient to the other. Don't let anyone tell you otherwise.

MAJOR POINTS TO REMEMBER

- There is a logical relationship between the existing state of knowledge about your topic and how you finally formulate a problem for study.
- The literature directs your overall purpose, which logically suggests a design type, which suggests your best means to an end.
- Questions can be asked and answered.
- Hypotheses are educated hunches that conjecture and are substantiated or refuted.
- A null hypothesis argues that the original hypothesis is erroneous and that whatever difference or association it proposes is accidental, not real/true/accurate.
- Hypotheses and questions both serve as a concrete reference point for all future action, including analysis.

EXERCISES

Challenge Yourself

1. Develop a question to study in your area of interest. From that question develop a proposition to test.

2. Then, challenge yourself: *Just how educated is that hunch? From where did you get enough knowledge to make such a hunch?*
3. Could you defend that proposition? Could you point to a body of knowledge to support it? If so, then developing a hypothesis-driven study may be legitimate. If you feel shaky, you might review the literature again to see if you can strengthen your case—or you may just need to back up and work from a question.

Exercise Your Null Hypothesis

Take a few minutes to practice formulating null hypotheses. Write down five hypotheses and for each one, formulate its null version. Remember, it's not the opposite of an original hypothesis; it simply states that what the hypothesis proposes isn't so.

Chapter 4

Variables

(A Fancy Term for a Simple Idea)

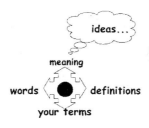

INTRODUCTION

Variables are simply factors that become objects of examination. If variation in age is of interest, then it's a variable. Is gender of interest? Education? Number of siblings? Diagnosis? Work setting? Ethnicity? Religion? Work history? Language? Anxiety? Age? Height? Whatever factors have capacity for variation can be conceptualized and studied as variables.

DEFINING VARIABLES

Research defines variables in two ways: *conceptually* (the actual concept itself) and *operationally* (indicators that tell us when we're seeing that variable in action). For some concepts, such as education or even religious affiliation, developing an operational definition isn't difficult. For more complex concepts (constructs) we have choices about where to start (the conceptual definition) as well as where to end (operational definition). For example, human development has been conceptualized and thus theorized in many ways, from physical to psychosexual to psychosocial to moral to cognitive to gender, to name but a few theoretical viewpoints. For constructs, then, you start by choosing which theoretical paradigm to use *for purposes of your study, and then you develop the operational definition from that paradigm.*

Say you choose a conceptual definition of aggression based on a certain social theory; its operational definition will then consist of the *indicators* (concrete and observable behaviors) used by that theory to talk about nature and degrees of aggression. In social work research many constructs are of interest; the challenge is to develop operational definitions that are neither overly simplistic nor reckless. There was a time when ear shape was considered a valid indicator of intelligence, for example.

Consider the following statement:

Male social workers publish more than female social workers.

What do you mean, exactly, by "publish"? What is your operational definition? How will you know it when you see it (its indicators)? Sound like a stupid question? Not really. You might mean professional work only, or you might want to include any kind of publishing, such as popular work outside the profession as well. Be specific.

Do you trust your therapist?
X therapy is an effective treatment tool for autistic children.
Are you satisfied with this program?
Religion has an impact in shaping family life.

What do you mean, exactly, by *trust,* by *effective treatment tool,* by *satisfied,* by *religion?* How are you operationalizing each one? What are their indicators?

Begin by "picking out" the most important variables of your research question as it is phrased and for each, ask yourself:

1. What do I mean, exactly, by this variable?
2. In what way do I want to think about/study (measure) this variable?
3. How precise do I want or need to be with this variable?

In studies that standardize the data-collection instrument, operational definitions are necessary precisely in order to pre-fix the questions—to make them specific, closed-ended, clear, and capable of capturing a full range of possible variation. Exploratory studies that seek to identify the important variables obviously can't define the terms as precisely. Still, becoming *as focused as you can* about the object of your interest is useful to either study process. Imagine asking someone your research question or stating your hypothesis and his or her asking for every term in that statement, *What do you mean, exactly?* How would you respond?

Dependent/Independent Variables

An *independent* variable is manipulated in a cause-and-effect experiment in order to examine its impact. It's also referred to as X or the *cause*. You impose it or offer it in order to test its effect. It might be a special treatment or service, a particular experience, the use of a certain drug, etc.

A *dependent* variable, traditionally referred to as Y or the *effect,* varies as a result of $X,$ whatever that is, and it is that variation you wish to study. You might be interested in studying variation in skill as a result of the special treatment or service, variation in attitude or knowledge as a result of the particular experience, or change in medical condition as a result of using a drug, etc. (See Chapter 9 for more on these types of variables.)

MEASURING VARIABLES

Although this discussion is usually found in the analysis section of research textbooks, there's value in learning about it earlier, as you think about the variables contained in your study and the instrument you will use to carry it out.

In quantitative studies that require statistics, variables are also said to be *measured* at one or other *level* (referred to as LOM, for level of measure). Some can only be measured at a certain level; others can be measured at any one of four possible levels. In effect, to measure a variable is to break it down into the ways you want to look at it in order to study its variation. Sometimes that breakdown is self-evident. For example, eye color can be only measured (broken down) by category of color. Education might be broken down (measured) in various ways. One study might ask if participants completed college. One might ask if they have completed any college classes at all. One might ask about type of school, such as public or private. One might ask respondents to rate the quality of their education compared to that of their peers. One might ask about number of years of education, and so on. How a variable is measured (broken down), depends on the nature and quantity of information about it that's needed by the study.

Nominal

When you measure (break down) a variable in terms of categories you're said to be measuring it at the nominal LOM. A breakdown of Christian, Muslim, Jewish, and "other" categories for *religion,* for example, or Democrat, Republican, Independent, and "other" for *political affiliation* reflects nominal LOM. A breakdown of response options such as yes/no, favor/oppose, and agree/disagree also reflects this LOM. Thus, some variables can be measured only at this level, broken down in terms of their various categories; some we choose to measure this way.

Ordinal

The ordinal level measures (breaks down) a variable in terms of degrees of difference rather than categorical differences, rank ordering attributes (variation) from low to high (socioeconomic status, for example) or least to most (*not at all, somewhat, very,* etc.). Rating scales measure variables at the ordinal LOM: numbers are used to reflect degree of difference but only conceptually; they can't be used with any precision. For instance, on a rating scale of 1 to 5 you can't logically say that whoever circled 4 is twice as satisfied with your program as whoever circled 2, only that the person must be quite a bit (an imprecise quantity) more satisfied. Or you can't say that whoever checked off "very useful" is X times as pleased as whoever checked off "somewhat useful." There is difference between them (variation), but the quantity is imprecise, only conceptual.

Interval

When a variable doesn't have inherent numerical properties (age does/intelligence does not; height does/self-esteem does not), but we choose to break it down and express it in quantitative terms anyway, we're measuring it at the interval level. Many variables of interest to social science in general and social work in particular are of this type, and using numbers to study them can help us understand their influence.

Major standardized tests, such as IQ, aptitude, college entrance, and many others that score people on such variables as self-esteem, satisfaction, intelligence, depression, etc., use this LOM. Here, the numbers mean more than those used in a rating scale, because intervals between one and two or sixty and sixty-one are exactly alike. However, the variables are not inherently numerical; we simply use numbers once again to try to understand them, but those numbers have no true zero point. Consider four scores on a test for depression:

Client 1 scores 80 (high)
Client 2 scores 75
Client 3 scores 50
Client 4 scores 20 (low)

Yes, client 1 scored four times as high as client 4, but you cannot say that client 1 is *four times as depressed* as client 4. It's not logical to speak about depression in this way.

Take a look at another example, a test about bigotry:

Mr. X scores 700 (high)
Ms. Y scores 100 (low)

Yes, Mr. X is much more bigoted than Ms. Y, but he's not *seven times more* bigoted. It doesn't make sense to speak about bigotry in this way. We can only say that he scored seven times as high.

So, we use the interval LOM to quantify the study of a variable that is not in and of itself numerical, but we choose to treat it as if it were. Finally,

> Outdoor temperature 1 is 80 degrees F
> Outdoor temperature 2 is 20 degrees F

However, temperature 1 is *not four times warmer* than temperature 2; only the numerical interval is four times greater.

Ratio

To break down such variables as income, age, height, number of home visits, years in practice or of education, number of clients, birth rate, etc., into their numerical properties is to measure them at the ratio LOM. Because the variable itself is numerical in nature, the numbers used to break it down are also real with a true zero point. Someone 66 inches tall *is* twice as tall as someone 33 inches tall; at 200 pounds someone *is* twice as heavy as a person at 100 pounds; a caseload of fifty clients *is* five times greater than one of ten.

The ratio LOM is considered the most "sophisticated" because when it comes time for statistical testing to examine the significance of quantitative results, using numbers with real meaning permits the most powerful tests.

MAJOR POINTS TO REMEMBER

- Variables are factors that you decide to make the object of study.
- Variables are defined at two levels: conceptual and operational.
- Operational definitions help us "see" the variable in action (in "operation").
- A major challenge of giving operational definitions to complex concepts is to keep those definitions valid.
- Variables are measured at four levels: nominal, ordinal, interval, and ratio.
- Sometimes the level at which we should measure a variable is self-evident; sometimes we can choose. The level selected re-

flects the nature and quantity of information desired for the study about that variable.

EXERCISES

Self-Test Number 1

1. Use a few sentences to write down your research topic in general terms.
2. Look it over and in specific terms develop a hypothesis or question.
3. Circle the factor(s) in that hypothesis or question that you are choosing to study. These are your variables.
4. How will you operationalize them? (How will you "know" them when you "see" them?) Be specific. If someone could ask what you mean by one of your variables, it's not specific enough.

Self-Test Number 2

Ask yourself: Just how focused do I need to be in order to get the information to answer my research question? Keep refining your thinking until your research hypothesis or question expresses exactly what you intend.

Self-Test Number 3

1. For each of the variables you have identified, develop a question or item you might put on a questionnaire along with response options. For each one, identify its LOM. Are you asking for categorical responses? Are you asking for degree of difference? Would it make sense to give each response a score, such as multiple choice with first response = 1 point, second response = 2 points, third response = 3 points, etc.? Are you asking about something that has real numerical meaning?
2. Provide a rationale for measuring each variable at that particular LOM.

Chapter 5

Assumptions

(Take Note! They Can Make an Ass of U and Me)

KEY CONCEPTS

beliefs
knowledge
opinions
proposition
research

INTRODUCTION

Similar to hypotheses, assumptions are propositions, but rather than test them you decide to take them as givens for the purpose of your study. Your hypothesis is a proposition to be studied; your assumptions are propositions to take for granted. Do all studies make assumptions? Pretty much. Assumptions put studies into context, helping others to understand your mind-set as you begin—where you're "coming from."

Consider the following hypothesis:

Social workers holding MSW (master of social work) degrees with professional education in the social group work method are more likely to catalyze mutual-aid dynamics in their group work practice than MSWs without such education.

The basic assumption in this study is that education has an impact on practice. This assumption is rooted in the research in and our knowledge of the impact of education on human behavior.

Now consider this question:

> How do practitioners incorporate grief work into their practice with recovering alcoholics?

The assumption here is that some practitioners do, in fact, incorporate grief work into their treatment. So the problem in this study is *how* they do it. Here, the researcher will select a sample of persons able to describe how grief work is incorporated into their treatment program. (These might be practitioners who use grief work or clients who have been in treatment that includes grief work, for example.)

Now compare that with this question:

> Do practitioners incorporate grief work into their practice with recovering alcoholics?

This question makes no assumptions about the inclusion of grief work. Instead, it wonders if grief work is even incorporated into treatment; it "backs up" from the previous question. This researcher, then, will select a sample of practitioners who work with persons in recovery and ask them *if* (not how) they incorporate grief work into their practice. If the literature indicates that some practitioners do include grief work in this type of treatment, then it's safe to ask how they do so. However, if the literature doesn't, then the *if they do* question needs to be asked first.

TYPES OF ASSUMPTIONS

There are basically four types of assumptions, some of which, as you'll quickly see, are safer (more acceptable) to make than others:

from previous research from knowledge of the subject }	formed by reviewing the literature
from belief systems from opinions }	formed by psychosociocultural life experience

Clearly, the assumptions that carry the greatest weight (thus the least likely to be challenged) are those rooted in research and knowledge. Ask yourself then, *What, if anything, am I taking for granted as I begin this study?* Are you asking a "how" question when perhaps the current state of our knowledge in the topic area suggests that you should ask an "if" question? Think about how reasonable your assumptions are; what may seem so to you (e.g., *all people value material ownership*) may not seem so to others. Strong enough criticism of your assumptions can disavow your entire study.

MAJOR POINTS TO REMEMBER

- Similar to a hypothesis, an assumption is a proposition but one to be taken as a given rather than tested.
- Assumptions need to be acknowledged and specified at the beginning of study.
- Assumptions come from one of four sources: research, knowledge, belief systems, and opinions.
- Assumptions help to put a study into context.
- Strong enough criticism of assumptions can disavow an entire study.

EXERCISE

Test Yourself

1. Review your research topic.
2. Write down your question or hypothesis.
3. Identify the inherent assumptions in it.
4. Talk to others who are knowledgeable about the subject. Do they think your assumptions are reasonable? Why or why not?
5. Review your question or hypothesis and change what needs to be changed in order to keep assumptions reasonable. This may mean, as in the previous example, "backing up" into a more basic question or hypothesis.

Chapter 6

Design Options

(So, What's the Overall Strategy?)

KEY CONCEPTS

asking questions
association
correlation
description
design as strategy
examining relationships
experimentation
exploration
hypothesis testing
purpose

INTRODUCTION

Design is a strategy for implementing your study, your guide for all you do from now on. In a nutshell, the function of design is to provide you with guidelines for answering your research question with the least amount of effort, time, and money.

FROM PURPOSE TO DESIGN

There are four basic purposes for research, each of which logically leads to a particular design type. As you formulate a problem and think about its importance, some kind of logical design framework is probably already beginning to choose you, whether you know it or not!

Purpose Number 1: Is Anything Going on Here?

This question calls for *exploratory* design. Its overarching purpose is to gain familiarity with a new or as yet unexplored phenomenon or to achieve new insights into one with which there's already some familiarity but not from the angle you have in mind. We may know much about alcoholism in some groups but not among the elderly, for example. It's conceivable, then, that a study of alcoholism among the elderly would be exploratory, yet a similar study of a group about which we know more would be another design.

Purpose Number 2: What **Exactly** *Is Going on Here?*

With *descriptive* design the assumption is that something is happening; hence, its purpose is to describe what that is, as if taking a snapshot. You might describe many things, such as characteristics of an individual or situation (as in a descriptive case example) or group (e.g., a particular segment of a client population) or process (e.g., counseling interaction) or problem (e.g., components of a community conflict) or environment (such as the physical layout of a factory) or even the characteristics of a relationship.

Purpose Number 3: Actually, I Think X Causes Y.

The main purpose of *experimental* design is to test a hypothesis (hunch) that something *(X)* causes something else *(Y)*. In this case, the literature offers you enough knowledge to formulate a cause-and-effect hunch (pretty bold!) and enough control on the entire research process to impose or offer something and test its effect.

Purpose Number 4: Well, Perhaps X Doesn't Cause Y, but I Think They're Associated.

The chief purpose of *correlational* design is to test association between variables. It's an attempt to approximate real experiments when you can't control the entire process—can't realistically or ethically cause something to happen and then test its effect or can't randomly assign people into an experimental or control group. It's also referred to as *quasi-experimental* design to connote the fact that it uses the same principles as experiments but with less control. Similar to experiments, correlational studies always work from a hypothesis, but experiments take place in lab settings, whereas correlational studies take place in the "real" world.

CONSTRUCTIVE COMBINATIONS

Does it seem as if more than one fit is possible for the study you have in mind? It's common to have exploration in a descriptive study or to have some description in an experiment. What differentiates them is their overarching purpose, and the label comes from where *you* place the emphasis. Studies with combined labels, as in *exploratory descriptive,* are common.

CONNECTIONS GIVE DIRECTION

The state of current knowledge, derived from reading the literature, helps you reach a purpose for study by revealing which questions have already been answered, which areas need more probing, and from which perspective a deeper look into a particular territory would be most useful. Once you know your purpose a design type becomes rather obvious, the occasional fly in the ointment being feasibility. For example, if your study's purpose suggests a descriptive study that observes schoolchildren in class every day over six months would yield the richest data but the real world impinges with time or cost or accessibility issues, etc., then another design needs to be used.

MAJOR POINTS TO REMEMBER

- Design is a strategy for implementing your study, a guide for all future action.
- Each of the four basic purposes for research logically leads to a particular design type.
- The purpose of exploratory design is to ask if anything is going on.
- The purpose of descriptive design is to ask what *exactly* is going on.
- The purpose of experimental design is to test cause and effect.
- The purpose of correlational design is to test association.
- Design types may have similarities but are differentiated by their overarching purpose. Elements of different designs are commonly combined in a single study.
- The state of current knowledge logically suggests a purpose for study by indicating which questions have been answered and which need further probing.

EXERCISE

Try It on for Size

1. Develop a research question for your topic of interest that reflects an exploratory design.
2. Develop a question or hypothesis in your topic of interest that is descriptive in nature.
3. Develop a cause-and-effect hypothesis related to your interest area that would take place in a lab setting.
4. Develop a hypothesis that is not cause and effect but that seeks in the "real world" (i.e., outside a lab setting) to test association of two variables in your interest area.

Chapter 7

Exploratory Design

(Is Anything Going on out There?)

KEY CONCEPTS

case study
exploration
nonrandom sample
reliability
reviewing literature
survey
validity

INTRODUCTION

The purpose of *exploratory* design is to become familiar with a new phenomenon or to gain new insights into it. That is, we don't know much about the topic of interest, either in general or from a particular angle in which we're interested, so we need to "explore" it.

WHEN TO USE IT

Exploratory studies can stand on their own, such as ethnography, but often precede further study into the same phenomenon. When you read about the three common approaches to exploring, you'll immediately understand why.

Exploratory studies always work from a question, because you don't have enough knowledge to formulate an educated hunch to test. Because they call for much intuitive reasoning and conceptualization, they're often thought of as the most artistic of the four design types. We have little knowledge to build on, so we rely on intuition to choose a direction of research and on our ability to conceptualize in order to identify potential variables.

THREE COMMON APPROACHES

There are three common ways of conducting exploratory studies; what they all have in common is the emphasis on fleshing out potentially important variables.

1. *Reviewing the literature:* Literature, both professional and popular, and from both within and without the profession is used to formulate variables, i.e., factors, to study further. Reviewing the literature can be a study in and of itself, but it is also the first step of all research, regardless of design type.
2. *Surveying relevant people:* People with practical experience with the area of interest are interviewed. You're looking for current insights and ideas, and you contact people who might be able to provide them. Similar to a literature review, your aim is to formulate variables as leads for study, but your focus is on the here and now rather than on the written word, which can include study of the past as well.
3. *Case study:* Here you carry out an intensive study of some selected examples that either reflect or are related to the problem of interest. You seek out and analyze selected instances of the phenomenon you're exploring that seem relevant. Sigmund Freud's intensive study of a few patients to gain theoretical insights and Carol Stack's long-term participant observation of inner-city kinship networks are good examples of this strategy. Sometimes experts and cases are one and the same, for example, asking social work practitioners to talk about their practice

makes them both the object of your study (cases) and experts (on their practice).

OVERVIEW OF METHOD

- The sample is nonrandom (See Chapter 15) because your goal is access to information, not generalization.
- Data collection (see Chapter 16) is generally flexible in order to ensure access to information, and it's usually carried out with instruments that seek qualitative (narrative) data.
- The measurement concepts of reliability and validity (see Chapter 14) speak primarily to methods and are demonstrated through what is referred to as a "thick" (i.e., very comprehensive and detailed) description of the entire study process.
- Analysis of the content (see Chapter 18) consists of using some model to make meaning of narrative material.

MAJOR POINTS TO REMEMBER

- The overarching purpose of *exploratory* design is to become familiar with a new phenomenon or to gain new insights into it.
- Exploratory studies can stand on their own but often precede further study into the same phenomenon.
- Exploratory studies always work from a question rather than hypothesis because you don't have enough knowledge to formulate an educated hunch to be tested.
- The strategies all emphasize looking for potentially important variables as food for thought.
- Three common exploratory strategies are reviewing the literature, interviewing people for current insights and ideas, and analyzing case studies.

EXERCISE

Check Closer for Fit

Refer to the exploratory question you developed in Chapter 6. Expand on the process of carrying out an exploratory study by using the previous three strategies as your guide. For each, how would you begin the study process? What types of literature might you read, for example? Who might be the experts, and where might you find them? What kinds of persons might provide case studies, and how might you gain access to them?

Chapter 8

Descriptive Design

(Taking a Snapshot)

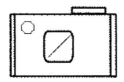

KEY CONCEPTS

description
generalization
inference
population
random sampling
sample

INTRODUCTION

A descriptive design portrays characteristics, both static and dynamic, and works from either a question or a hypothesis, depending on the state of current knowledge. The less information you have the less you can formulate a hypothesis (such as, *More men than women . . .*), hence, the more logical to work from a question (*Do more men than women . . . ?*). Common descriptive subjects are characteristics of a group, place, situation, and process.

Mind-Set

Descriptive studies are interested in generalization (making inferences from a small group [sample] to the larger group from which the sample was drawn [its population]). Thus, the concepts of *measure-*

ment and *random sampling* are important (see Chapters 14 and 15, respectively). Measurement refers to the reliability and validity of the instrument (measurement) for study. Random sampling is a method of selecting cases to study that gives each one an equal chance of being included. Random sampling is important to descriptive study because it helps prevent bias in the final sample and thus permits generalization from it to the larger group of interest.

WHEN TO USE IT

Descriptive design is called for when your overall aim is to describe a phenomenon, as in a physical environment, types of case records, amount and nature of postgraduate training of social workers in a particular state, characteristics of a relationship, demographics, types of behaviors, nature of attitudes, level of knowledge, etc.

Descriptive studies are sometimes regarded as not very useful or simply boring. In fact, there's a great deal of room and need for descriptive studies in social work, which, in order to be effective, must carry out its mandates based on reality, not on beliefs or assumptions we make about reality. It's all too easy to think we know, for example, (that *so* many more women than men attend the program or that we offer X service *so* much more than Y service or that the needs of a particular community are *this* not *that* or that people in *this* group always behave in *that* way, etc. In fact, descriptive studies are often referred to as "corrective experiences" precisely because they help us correct our perceptions, which are too often inaccurate, if only because we rarely have the chance to see a picture in toto.

OVERVIEW OF METHOD

- The sample (see Chapter 15) is random because the purpose of this design type is to generalize. Furthermore, the larger the sample the better. Generally, a sample of thirty cases is considered the minimum.
- Data collection (see Chapter 16) is predetermined and unchangeable, both as to the use of a standardized instrument and the testing process.

- The measurement concepts of reliability and validity (see Chapter 14) speak to the integrity of the instrument. Reliability refers to its consistent ability to obtain the same data under the same circumstances. Validity refers to its ability to tap only into whatever you want to measure.
- Analysis (see Chapter 19) consists primarily of statistical analysis of quantitative data.

MAJOR POINTS TO REMEMBER

- A descriptive design portrays characteristics and works from either a question or a hypothesis, depending on the state of current knowledge.
- Descriptive studies are interested in generalization, drawing inferences about a large population of interest from a sample.
- Random sampling and measurement are central to descriptive design.
- Descriptive studies can contribute a great deal to our understanding by providing what's often referred to as "corrective experiences."

EXERCISE

Check Closer for Fit

Refer to the descriptive problem you formulated in the exercise at the end of Chapter 6. Use it to formulate a question or hypothesis around the following four possibilities that you believe, if asked or tested, would advance our knowledge in your topic area:

1. A group
2. A place
3. A situation
4. A process

Chapter 9
Experimental Design
(This Causes That . . . I *Think!*)

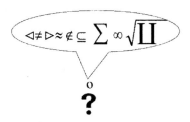

KEY CONCEPTS

cause
control
dependent variable
effect
experiment
group difference
independent variable
plausible alternative explanations
posttest
pretest
random sampling
statistical significance

INTRODUCTION

The purpose of experimental design is to test a hypothesis regarding some cause-and-effect relationship (a hypothesis of *group difference*). In contrast to descriptive design, which aims to describe, experimental design seeks to explain.

WHEN TO USE IT

An experimental design is appropriate when you meet all three of these criteria:

1. There's a great deal of knowledge about the topic—enough, in fact, to support an educated guess about causation. That's pretty educated!
2. You can actually manipulate whatever you believe to be a "cause" (subject people to it or offer it to them) in order to examine its "effect" (as in a treatment method or drug or experience).
3. You can control who does or doesn't get that "cause" (who does/does not get your treatment or take a certain drug or participate in a particular experience).

In some ways this design type is the opposite of exploratory design, used when you have very little information.

CONCEPTS BASIC TO THIS DESIGN

- A *cause* (*X* or *independent* variable) occurs both before and independently of anything else. You can manipulate it in such a way as to impose it on or offer it to others to study its effects. It occurs/exists first, *independently* of anything else.
- An *effect* (*Y* or *dependent* variable) occurs as a result of a cause. Its variation, or how it looks as a result of your cause, is what you're interested in examining.
- An *experimental group* is subjected to or offered *X*, whatever it is.
- A *control group* is not subjected to or offered *X*. It may be subjected to or get nothing or something other than *X* (such as another drug, a placebo, a different treatment type, etc.).

   Control groups are used to help protect against the possibility that something other than *X* caused *Y* (called *plausible alternative explanations;* see Chapter 11). Here's how. A group of people is invited to participate in an experiment. Using a random sampling method (Chapter 15) people are assigned into either the experimental or control group. The experimental group gets your *X*, whatever it is; the control group doesn't (it gets nothing or something else or a placebo). If at the end of the experiment (the end of your *X*) the two groups differ on what you're testing (say, skill level) more than probability theory (chance) would suggest, you can substantiate your hypothesis. If not, you can't.

Your challenger asks, how do you know that such and such wasn't the reason your experimental group did better on skill. Well, whatever the experimental group experienced in the world during the program the control group also experienced and the difference is still significant; so we can rule out that possibility. That is, if the differences between the two groups at posttest are significant (as revealed by statistical testing), then you can say that they're real/true/accurate, not just an artifact of chance or some unknown factor.

- *Random sampling* is a method of sampling that allows probability to dictate who or what will end up in your final sample. It provides a basic safeguard against sample bias and allows you to estimate the degree of sample error that is, in fact, present.

The Basic Experiment: Before and After with Two Groups

	Experimental Group	Control Group
Pretested?*	Yes	Yes
Subjected to *X*?	Yes	No
Posttested?*	Yes	Yes

OVERVIEW OF METHOD

- Random sampling (see Chapter 15) is used to assign members into either the experimental or control group.
- Design must include the introduction of rigorous controls to eliminate all plausible alternative explanations (see Chapter 11).

---

*Using the same measurement tool, the two groups are assessed through statistical analysis for similarities and differences.

- Data collection (see Chapter 16) is predetermined and unchangeable, both as to the use of a standardized instrument and the testing process.
- The measurement concepts of reliability and validity (see Chapter 14) speak to the integrity of the instrument. Reliability refers to its consistent ability to obtain the same data under the same circumstances. Validity refers to its ability to tap into whatever you want to measure and nothing but that.
- Analysis (see Chapters 19, 20, and 21) consists primarily of analyzing descriptive and inferential statistics.

Three Criteria to Show Causation

1. X and Y must fit together (covary).
2. X (cause) must be able to precede Y (effect); logical, yes?
3. You're satisfied that no other plausible explanations exist for what you find (see Chapter 11).

Consider the following hypothesis:

Smoking (X) causes lung cancer (Y).

To claim causality you must show that you always need X (smoking) for Y (lung cancer) to occur and that X (smoking) is sufficient for Y (lung cancer) to occur. So, to substantiate this hypothesis we need to find that smoking is both necessary and sufficient for lung cancer to occur. Today, it's commonly agreed that smoking is enough to cause lung cancer, but there's still some disagreement as to whether it's necessary for lung cancer to occur, since nonsmokers are known to get lung cancer.

Finally, remember that hypotheses are only substantiated, never proven. We can never completely rule out the possibility that some factor other than X caused Y. Even if we can show causation, it's always tentative and subject to later revision, only viable until later evidence suggests something different. In fact, this kind of design is often used to do just that—to refute "old" theories in favor of new ones.

MAJOR POINTS TO REMEMBER

- The purpose of experimental design is to test a hypothesis regarding cause and effect.
- An experimental design is appropriate when there's a great deal of knowledge about the topic, when you can formulate a hypothesis and manipulate whatever you believe to be a cause to examine its effect, and when you can control who does/does not get subjected to that cause.
- A *cause* refers to something that you can manipulate in such a way as to impose it on or offer to others.
- An *effect* occurs as a result of a cause; its variation is what you examine.
- An *experimental group* is subjected to or offered the cause. A *control group* is not subjected to or offered the cause.
- Using a control group helps to protect against plausible alternative explanations.
- If at the end of the experiment the two groups differ on the effect more than probability theory would dictate, you can substantiate your hypothesis.
- Using random sampling to assign subjects (cases) into one of the two groups protects against sample bias and allows sample error estimation.
- The basic experiment form includes pretest, manipulation of X to the experimental but not the control group, and posttest.
- Three criteria for showing causation are that cause and effect must covary, that cause precedes effect, and that no other plausible alternative explanations account for posttest differences.
- To claim causality the cause must be both necessary and sufficient for the effect to occur.

EXERCISE

Check Closer for Fit

Imagine the opportunity to carry out an experiment in your area of interest and formulate a cause-and-effect hypothesis. How would such an experiment look? Would it be realistic? Would it be feasible? What might be some obstacles in implementation, and how might you overcome them?

Chapter 10

Correlational Design

(Actually, I Don't Know If This Causes That, but They Sure Seem to "Go" Together)

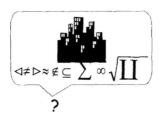

KEY CONCEPTS

association
control
correlation
ex post facto
hypothesis of association
longitudinal
plausible alternative explanations
quasi-experimental
relational

INTRODUCTION

The purpose of correlational studies is to test *association;* they're "real world" attempts to approximate experiments when we don't have control over X—when we can't realistically or ethically cause something to happen in order to test the results. These studies are always framed around a hypothesis.

WHEN TO USE IT

A correlational study might examine association between variables in one group, such as body image and ethnicity in a group of young adult women (cross-sectional). It might examine association between two groups, such as middle-aged and young adult women, around a variable of interest, such as body image (comparison). Or it might examine the impact of time on some variable, such as the long-term impact of an eight-week group treatment on attitude and behavior (longitudinal).

Many relationships can be studied only this way. We can't cause someone to become alcoholic or depressed in order to study the effects, but current knowledge suggests some association. So then what? So we find a way to study the experiences of people who fit the profile of interest—people who are alcoholic or depressed or victims of a natural disaster or children of divorce, etc. Then, if we find the presence of depression in alcoholic persons, we don't say alcoholism causes depression but, rather, isn't it interesting that when one is present the other seems to be too? Thus, we carry out a study not with an aim of cause and effect but strength and intensity of a relationship. Ultimately, we might even infer some possible explanations depending on the weight of the results.

Correlational studies are also referred to as quasi-experimental to connote the fact that they use the same principles as experiments but admittedly with less control.

CORRELATION

When association exists and covariance of variables is in the same direction ("more" of both or "less" of both), correlation is said to be positive. When covariance exists but takes the variables in opposing directions ("more" of one and "less" of the other), it is said to be negative. Thus, if self-esteem in sixth-grade girls is higher after participating in a special school program, then self-esteem and participation in that program have a positive correlation. If image is lower, they have a negative correlation. Both positive and negative correlation can range from very weak to very strong (presented statistically as *correlation coefficients*). Obviously, the stronger the correlation the stronger the association.

FOUR COMMON APPROACHES

Ex Post Facto

An ex post facto ("after the fact") strategy measures (studies) the effect of an event after it has occurred, such as a hostage situation or airplane crash or large-scale blackout or natural disaster. Clearly, we couldn't cause any one of these things to happen, but their impact is of interest.

Strategy

Is there a group (victims of an earthquake) to be studied?	Yes
Is there a pretest measurement to make?	No
Is there an *X* (the earthquake) to study?	Yes
Is there a posttest measurement (psychological impact) to make*	Yes

Strengths and Weaknesses

This strategy allows us to study the effects of phenomena that cannot be studied by experiment. It lacks a control group but comparison groups may be available. It lacks a pretest against which the ex post facto measure can be compared (no baseline). It consists of an accidental sample, which, however, might be random sampled for a final sample to study, making the study more wieldy and allowing generalization from the sample to the larger group. You can't safely generalize to other groups, however.

Before and After with One Group

This design strategy is used when you can pretest a group before introducing *X*, whatever it is, such as a group treatment program.

---

*Using the same instrument, the group is assessed through statistical analysis for similarities and differences.

Strategy

Is there a group (adolescent clients) to be studied?	Yes
Is there a pretest measurement (attitude) to make?*	Yes
Is there an X (e.g., a ten-week group program) to test?	Yes
Is there a posttest measurement (attitude) to make?*	Yes

Strengths and Weaknesses

Major strengths are the potential for a pretest and thus baseline data against which to compare posttest results, and control over who gets subjected to X, allowing the possibility of a random sample and reducing the potential for bias. Not having a control or comparison group, however, still leaves one to wonder if X rather than some unknown factor caused the results.

Before and After with Two Groups

This strategy is used with access to a matching (comparison) group (as in two groups of teens, one of which participates in a ten-week program). Random sampling people/cases into the groups may be possible; if not, you match the groups closely around important characteristics. Then, differences that exist are revealed at pretest and can be factored into analysis.

	Experimental Group	**Control Group**
Pretested?*	Yes	Yes
Subjected to X	Yes	No
Posttested?*	Yes	Yes

Strengths and Weaknesses

This strategy most closely approximates a true experiment. Its strengths are the ability to manipulate X (offering a service to some and not to others), the collection of baseline data against which to compare posttest results, and a comparison group to help protect

---

*Using the same instrument, the group is assessed through statistical analysis for similarities and differences.

against plausible alternative explanations (see Chapter 11). Major weaknesses are that random sampling into the groups is not usually possible and that pretest differences between the experimental and only available comparison group may reveal differences that are too vast to permit any meaningful comparison.

Longitudinal Study

The goal of this strategy is to study the long-term impact, if any, of X. You can study only one group (an experimental group, subjected to X) or if a comparison group is available, two groups. The use of a comparison group helps to reduce the possibility that something other than X explains your findings (see Chapter 11). This example depicts the use of two groups.

Strategy

	Experimental Group	**Control Group**
Pretested?*	Yes	Yes
Subjected to X	Yes	No
Posttested time 1?*	Yes	Yes
Posttested time 2?*	Yes	Yes
Posttested time 3?*	Yes	Yes
Posttested time 4?*	Yes	Yes
Posttested time 5?*	Yes	Yes

In this example the groups are posttested five times, but *you* decide how often and how much for your study. If once a year for ten years makes sense to the purpose of your study and is feasible, do it. If once every three months for two years makes sense and is feasible, then do it. There are no set rules. Just remember that the longer the study, the more difficult to follow/find/keep participants.

Strengths and Weaknesses

This strategy permits a long-term look at the stability of X. Pre-testing allows a baseline measure against which to make posttest

---

*Using the same measurement tool, the two groups are assessed through statistical analysis for similarities and differences.

measures. A comparison group reduces the potential for plausible alternative explanations (see Chapter 11).

A weakness that is not inherent in the design but often emerges with this strategy is the great potential for sample attrition.

OVERVIEW OF METHOD

- You try to introduce some degree of random sampling (see Chapter 15), such as taking a random sample from an existing accidental pool of possible sample members.
- Design must include consideration of plausible alternative explanations (see Chapter 11).
- Data collection (see Chapter 16) is predetermined and unchangeable, both as to the use of a standardized instrument and the testing process.
- The measurement concepts of reliability and validity (see Chapter 14) speak to the integrity of the instrument. Reliability refers to its consistent ability to obtain the same data under the same circumstances. Validity refers to its ability to tap into whatever you want to measure and nothing but that.
- Analysis (see Chapters 20 and 21) consists of statistical analysis of quantitative data using the language of correlation coefficients.

MAJOR POINTS TO REMEMBER

- The purpose of correlational studies is to test *association,* or how variables relate to each other, both in nature and strength.
- Correlational studies attempt to approximate real experiments when we can't realistically or ethically manipulate *X.*
- Correlational studies are often used to study the impact of major natural disasters or other phenomena (such as alcoholism, divorce, mental illness, etc.) that we would not cause in order to study but the results of which are interesting and important to understand.
- Correlational studies test hypotheses and are used when a strong enough knowledge base in the subject allows for an educated guess of association.

- Covariation of variables can be either positive or negative and range from very weak to very strong.
- As much use as possible of probability sampling increases the credibility of this design.
- Four common approaches are ex post facto, before and after with one group, before and after with two groups, and longitudinal.

EXERCISE

Check Closer for Fit

Refer to the correlational study you formulated in Chapter 6. Use that hypothesis to develop

1. a before-and-after study with one group;
2. a before-and-after study with one experimental and one comparison group; and
3. a longitudinal study of one group.

Chapter 11

Plausible Alternative Explanations

(How Do You Know It Wasn't . . .?)

> ...but how do
> you know it's
> because...?

KEY CONCEPTS

bias
comparison
control
rival explanation

INTRODUCTION

Other than a mouthful to say, plausible alternative explanations are hypothetical rival explanations for your findings. They apply most directly to experimental and correlational designs. How can you respond to these rivals? In effect, you try to eliminate them by anticipating them as the study is designed. Most of them are eliminated by using a control group (which means experiments, rather than correlational studies, have the best chance of really eliminating them).

HOW DO THEY FIT IN?

Say you're interested in tenant attitudes and wonder if an educational program would be effective in changing attitudes toward organizing. You locate a group of tenants and test them on attitudes toward tenant organization with a questionnaire (your pretest). You then offer them the educational program, and when it ends you administer the same questionnaire (your posttest).

Your results suggest that their attitudes toward organizing are much more positive after the program. Great! You prepare a report for a potential funding source, and just as you're getting ready to present it, along come a couple of killjoys who ask you how you know that the attitude change is really due to your program.

"How do you know some *external events* during your study (such as publicity about tenancy in the newspapers or on television) didn't cause the change in attitude?" asks one of them.

"Well," you respond, "we used a comparison group. We couldn't use a control group because we didn't conduct this study in a lab, but we did find a similar tenant group, and whatever external events might have occurred would have influenced both groups. Yet, when we posttested them we found a significant difference between them."

"I see," he says, "but how do you know your experimental group wasn't in some way unusual and perhaps especially susceptible to change without your program and so was *biased* to begin with?"

"Because," you answer, "not only did we choose our groups very carefully, but by pretesting both we saw that they're in fact very comparable. And so, again, even if our experimental group was biased, so was the control group, and the differences were still significant between them after the program."

"Well then," your interrogator continues, "how do you know that the attitudes of the experimental group didn't change simply because of all your *attention?*"

"A good point," you concede, "but one we thought about! We gave both groups attention—not the same kind, but both groups got attention," you respond with a smug smile.

Now your challengers are becoming rather impressed, so of course they seek to argue further.

"What about natural *maturation?*" asks the other killjoy rather haughtily. "How do you know that your experimental group didn't change simply because they matured during your program?"

"Well," you respond self-assuredly, "they probably did, but so did the members of the comparison group and, again, the differences between them after our program were still significant!"

Now the killjoys are really looking to trip you up!

"How about the fact that you *did* pretest everyone?" asks the other one slyly. "Taking the pretest could have started your experimental group thinking and caused the change."

"Oh, sure," you quickly agree, "but to eliminate this small possibility, we'd have needed to give up the chance to pretest, and we'd rather acknowledge the slight chance that pretesting may have had this effect. Anyway, if it did affect the experimental group, it also affected the comparison group, and the experimental group still did better at posttest."

Now the first one pipes in again.

"Well, isn't it possible that just being part of the testing process caused the changes? After all, they took the same test twice. Perhaps the changes are simply due to a *practice effect* . . ."

"That's true," you agree, "but, again, we thought this possibility was only slight and so chose the option of having baseline data."

Looking increasingly impressed by your thoughtfulness, he adds: "What if the members of your experimental group tried to *please you* with certain answers or to *outwit you* in some way with posttest answers?"

"Yes," you acknowledge,"that's always possible. We used slightly different versions of the same questionnaire to help prevent this kind of manipulation."

Finally, as if dredging up the last challenge, Killjoy 1 wonders if perhaps the *standards of analysis* at posttest weren't different from those at pretest (i.e., lower).

"Perhaps," he argues, "your observers were more tired, less enthusiastic, less careful at the end of the project than at the beginning. . . . Or in the converse, perhaps they were more skilled at posttest? Either way, a bias would be introduced, no?"

"Yes," you agree that these are possibilities. However," you reply, "we trained our researchers carefully and thoroughly."

Apparently convinced and very impressed by your thoroughness (but depressed by their inability to find obvious flaws in your study) the two killjoys prepare to leave. As they approach the door, Killjoy 2 stops and yells, "Aha! I just remembered that your report said about twenty-five percent of the experimental group dropped out before the end of the program! What about it?" he asks excitedly. "Maybe those who stayed were biased in some way and that's what caused your findings, not the program itself!"

"Uh-oh," you say. "That's a real possibility (i.e., plausible alternative explanation) that we didn't consider."

Then you ask yourself if you could have made the program shorter so that more people might have stayed. You're not sure. Could you have done more to convince people how important it was to the study to stay until the end? Probably. Oh well, live and learn . . .

The plausible alternative explanations identified in the previous scenario are the major ones that you need to attend to; check a comprehensive research textbook to identify others and to learn more about the details of eliminating them.

HOW BIG A WORRY ARE THEY?

In effect, plausible alternative explanations are as big a worry as you want to make them. You should *always* think about the validity of the data produced by your study. However, rival hypotheses are always considered at the outset of and integrated into the methods of any good experimental and correlational study. It's expected that experimental studies, which make the boldest claims (cause and effect), will introduce all rigor possible to reduce the threat of alternative explanations; clearly, it's less possible for correlational studies to do as much. The point here is, in a nutshell, that as many factors as possible that might have a significant influence on your findings should be considered so that if killjoys ask, "But could it have been such and such that accounted for the change?" you're well prepared to respond.

MAJOR POINTS TO REMEMBER

- Plausible alternative explanations are rival explanations for your findings.
- The more you can eliminate them, the more legitimate become claims of causality or association.
- Most plausible alternative explanations are eliminated by using a control or comparison group; some are mitigated by using different but equivalent pretest and posttest instruments; the threat of some is reduced by carefully training researchers and participants.
- The most common plausible alternative explanations are described and discussed in every research textbook.
- All experimental and correlational studies must attempt to eliminate as many rival explanations as possible.

EXERCISE

Do They Apply?

Refer to some of the hypotheses you've formed as practice exercises. For each one ask yourself these questions:

1. Can you identify some challenges in the form of those identified in this chapter that might come your way?
2. What might you do to reduce the threat of plausible alternative explanations in each case? What kind of actions (controls) would you need to introduce? Would they be feasible? Why or why not?
3. Would you need to change/revise the study in any way? How?

Chapter 12
Practice Evaluation
(Are You Doing Good Work or What?)

KEY CONCEPTS

clinical research
collaboration
effectiveness
experimental single-case study
idiographic study
intra-unit comparison
$N = 1$
single-subject design
single-system design
time
time-series design

INTRODUCTION

Practice evaluation (*clinical research, single-subject* or *single-system* or *time-series* design, $N = 1$, or *idiographic* or *experimental single-case* study) moves the practitioners away from theorizing about the value of what they do to critically study its impact on client systems. For this design, a system might be individuals, dyads, groups, or any entity that can be conceptualized as a system and for which goals can be expressed and progress can be tracked. If you study the effect of a certain therapy for couple's counseling, the *couple* is your system, and you measure how the couple progresses *as a couple*. If you study the impact of certain interventions on group cohesion, the *group* is your system, and you measure how the group fares *as a group*.

Clearly, some things (such as behavior) are easier to track than others, but the inventory of instruments to measure both complex processes and complex issues grows every day. In this design independent and dependent variables apply. The practice (treatment/service) you carry out is X (*independent* variable) and its effect (changes in mood states or behavior or skill) is Y (*dependent* variable).

In contrast to experiments or correlational studies, which make intergroup comparisons, this design is interested in *intrasystem* comparison—comparing a system with itself over time by tracking your intervention's impact on it. Its ultimate aim is not generalization but *replication*—to carry out enough similar studies to be able to draw inferences of effectiveness about a piece of practice (treatment/service). Yes, you can already discover some of that by examining its impact on one system, but the more you repeat it with other like systems and get the same results, the stronger your claims of effectiveness can be.

Mind-Set

The mind-set for practice evaluation is *collaboration*. We don't impose practice, and we don't impose practice evaluation. We explain purpose, contract around goals, request agreement, and invite close collaboration in conceptualizing, developing, implementing, and analyzing process and progress. In fact, this design is very complementary to practice. Note how the components of evaluation are very similar to those of practice.

Practice Evaluation	Practice
Specify the problem to examine (e.g., level of anxiety), which becomes *Y,* your *dependent* variable.	Identify and examine the problem(s) to be addressed.
Measure that problem (i.e., nature and frequency of symptoms) with an assessment tool.	Assess the problems in order to shape the course of treatment/service.
Specify the intervention to evaluate, including a proposed time frame. That becomes *X,* your *independent* variable.	Determine which treatment/service to implement, along with some understanding of time frame.
Assess changes in the nature of the problem over time using the tool originally employed.	Assess progress as treatment/service is carried out.

WHEN TO USE IT

This type of design is best suited to tracking symptoms that can be easily measured or observed. Thus, the more complex the dependent variable (the problem to be tracked), the more difficult it may be to partialize it into components that can be tracked easily and reliably (although as noted previously, increasingly good instruments are available).

OVERVIEW OF METHOD

Before treatment/service begins a measurement tool is selected (either an existing one or one developed specifically for this purpose) and *baseline measures* (this design's version of a pretest) of the problem *(Y)* are taken. Three to five measures are ideal, but even two can begin to build a visual pattern. Results are plotted on a graph, giving a picture before your intervention *(X)*. For example, a couple might track the number of fights they have each day before they begin their sessions, or you might rate group cohesion at the next meeting before introducing a particular intervention.

Treatment/service *(X)* begins, regular measurements of the system continue (status of the problem assessed), and the results are plotted on the graph. When and how often? *You* decide based on whatever makes sense.

At the end of the intervention, or at least at the end of its research component, you eyeball the graph for one of three possible correlations: *positive* (the more you intervened the better the system did); *negative* (the more you intervened the worse it did); or *no apparent correlation* (your intervention seems to have made no difference), which is arguably as bad an outcome as a negative correlation.

A FEW VARIATIONS

AB Design on One Variable

While talking about her problems, your client says she can't seem to stop crying. Together you decide to track her crying spells as one way of determining how she's feeling and if your treatment is helping her feel better. She's going to see you three times a week, and she's to keep track of her crying spells on a daily basis. At each visit you'll record on a graph the daily number of spells since the last visit and examine it together (Figure 12.1). Her first visit is scheduled for five days later, and she's to track her crying spells every day until her first visit as a baseline.

ABAB Design on One Variable

Continuing with the same scenario, let's say you go on vacation for two weeks. Rather than end the study, you and your client decide she'll continue to track her progress while you're away (A2).When you return you'll continue the treatment (B2) and also see how she did while you were away (Figure 12.2). This design is also known as *single-subject experiment* because A2 (when you're away) serves as a "case control" by reflecting what happens when *X* stops for any reason.

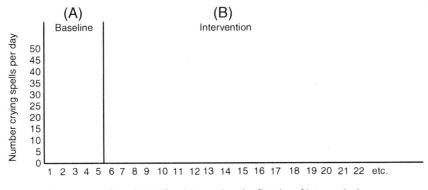

FIGURE 12.1. AB Design on One Variable

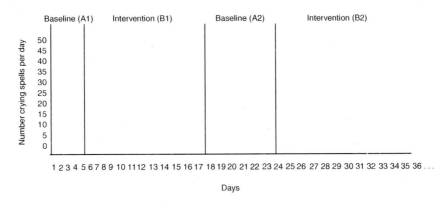

FIGURE 12.2. ABAB Design on One Variable (days 1-5 equal before intervention; 6-7 equal original intervention; 18-24 equal case control period; 25 plus equal renewed original intervention)

ABC Design

Another scenario: let's say you, your client, or both aren't satisfied with her progress. You consult with your supervisor and brainstorm another approach that includes structured daily homework. Your client agrees. Figure 12.3 shows what that graph looks like.

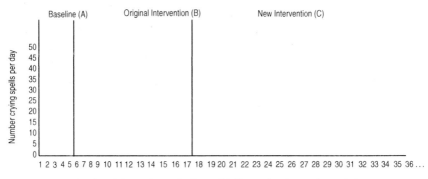

FIGURE 12.3. ABC Design

ANALYSIS

Eyeball the graph to see if a dramatic enough pattern exists to gauge success. If not (which is often the case) a simple statistical test can be used to examine if the difference between what would be expected (theoretical probability) and what really happened (reality) is significant.

CHOOSING THE SYSTEM

One way to guard against (your) biasing the project and a way to introduce some control into this design is to let probability dictate who or what will become your study system. For example, out of all the cases that fit the profile, use a random process to determine which person you'll invite to participate. Or decide that the next new case with the right profile that's presented to you (walks through the door, is referred, etc.) will be the one you invite.

ISSUES TO CONSIDER

1. Choice of client system, intervention *(X),* and problem to address *(Y)* must be logical and theoretically sound, not just seem like a good idea at the time.

2. Your goals (changes in *Y,* the dependent variable) must be reasonable.
3. Consider collecting quantitative or qualitative data (or both) and using any feasible collection method.
4. The measurement instrument must be stable (reliable), sensitive (valid), and fairly easy to use.
5. Rating can take place during practice or later.
6. Many sources of information can be considered. Who's the best source? The client system? You? Someone else? If so, who? A colleague? Family member? Teacher? Consider the study's purpose and the best source given the desired perspective. Consider triangulation (more than one source).
7. Have a time frame in mind, and think relatively short term. This design is not intended to be open-ended.
8. Think about bias, particularly yours. (You can see the potential for wanting to see progress where it may not exist, yes?)

MAJOR POINTS TO REMEMBER

- The purpose of single-system design is to measure change over time (i.e., intrasystem comparison); thus, time is always an element in this type of study.
- Systems might be individuals or groups or any entity that can be conceptualized as such and for which goals can be expressed and the process can be tracked.
- Practice (treatment/service) is the independent variable *(X)* in this design, and its effect (changes in mood states or behavior or skill) is the dependent variable *(Y)*.
- The ultimate aim of single-system design is replication, not generalization.
- The components of practice evaluation closely resemble those of practice.
- The mind-set for practice evaluation is collaboration, from conceptualization to analysis.
- Methodology consists of selecting a measurement tool, taking baseline measures, introducing an intervention, taking measures during that intervention, and analysis.

- Choices of client system, intervention, and desired outcome must have a logical and theoretical basis.
- All data-collection methods can be used. Either practitioner or client may act as rater, and rating can take place during actual practice or later.
- To select a source of information consider the study's purpose and perspective; triangulation may be a good option.
- The instrument used must be stable, sensitive, and fairly easy to use.
- The study should be relatively short term.
- Consider the potential for practitioner bias.
- This design is best suited to tracking symptoms that are easily measured or observed.
- The more you can let probability dictate who becomes your study system, the better.

EXERCISE

Ask Yourself

How might this design fit into the work you do?
1. Choose a client system from among your caseload.
2. Identify the general problem.
3. Select a dependent variable (i.e., a symptom of that problem you'd want to change).
4. Select an independent variable (i.e., the treatment/service you'd implement).
5. Select or develop the instrument you'd use to test changes in the dependent variable.
6 Develop a service or treatment process, including what you would do (exactly) and for how long.
7. Using a separate sheet of paper, plot an AB graph that would illustrate success.
8. Next plot an ABAB graph that would illustrate stabilization while you're away on vacation.
9. Finally, plot an ABC graph that would illustrate a change in treatment.

Chapter 13

Program Evaluation

(Just How Good *Are* We?)

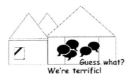

KEY CONCEPTS

accountability
assessment
consumer empowerment
documentation
evaluation
monitoring
politics

INTRODUCTION

Program evaluation is the study of many aspects of organizations, such as program design, planning, implementation, monitoring, and effectiveness (often referred to as outcome studies). The ultimate goal of program design is professional accountability, which goes hand in hand with consumer empowerment by making visible and even public who's doing what to whom; as well as how, how often, and why; and whether what's being done is meeting professional service mandates efficiently, effectively, and ethically (Smith, 1990).

Program evaluation includes questions about planning and design (before, during, or after), such as assessment of needs, goal appropriateness and achievement, design and development structures, nature of interventions required, and evaluation of achievement.

It also asks questions (before, during, or after) about quantity and quality of services offered, the nature of their implementation (e.g., the nature of service providers), projected or real successes and failures, possible design flaws, and costs. Outcome studies examine the impact of what we do, its effectiveness in real-world terms. In other words, are we really helping anyone?

Mind-Set

Michael Smith (1990) suggests four ways to think about program evaluation:

1. As a research *method,* which provides a scientifically accepted protocol for selecting a problem to study, selecting a design, obtaining a sample, collecting data, and analyzing results, helping to prevent biased or haphazard judgments
2. As a form of *practice* by rendering a service to an organization as a client—helping it examine its internal and external needs, health, and welfare
3. As a *field* of study, which assesses the quality of our social policies, programs, and interventions and offers special techniques for evaluating efficiency and effectiveness
4. As a *political process,* the methodological rigor of which helps to ensure that we're seen as objective investigators in the never ending political environment of competing needs, values, and ideologies

APPLYING DESIGN TYPES
TO PROGRAM EVALUATION

Exploration

Professionals involved in the services offered by the organization as well as literature that provides a history of service in a similar or related area can be helpful in program design and planning and even for evaluation purposes, such as comparing approaches to service. Interviewing employees with practical experience in a particular area of an organization can give you a flavor of the informal system, for example, or of professional and/or interdisciplinary dynamics or of organizational norms, cultures, and subcultures. Many subcultures exist in hospitals, for example, disciplines where several collaborate toward common goals. Finally, you might also carry out case studies, such as the intensive study of one department or one client group or one system of service.

Description

How many times have you believed one thing about an organization only to discover that you were wrong, wrong, wrong!? That's what a corrective experience is, and that's what descriptive studies provide. There's plenty of room for and value to program-related description of all kinds. You can focus on management or service providers or service consumers. You can look at an organization's internal environment (who's doing what to whom and how) or its external one (the larger context within which it operates, including physical, political, and economic climates).

If program evaluation is about professional accountability, then we need to keep track of what we're doing. If it's about consumer empowerment, then we need to *know* what we're doing, not operate on assumptions or beliefs.

Experimentation

The purpose of experimental design is to test cause and effect. So, can an experiment be carried out under the rubric of program evaluation? Think about your practice setting.

1. Do you have substantial knowledge about a topic of organizational interest? Is it enough to formulate a hypothesis? If so, move on.
2. Can you imagine *ethically* causing something (subjecting people in or related to the organization to your X or offering it to them) in order to examine its effect: a special program, a unique approach to service, a new policy, a new service provider, a revised intake or discharge process? If so, move on.

3. Can you imagine *ethically* controlling who would be subjected to or offered whatever you want to test? Management? Employees? Clients? Related others? If so, move on.
4. Can you imagine obtaining a control group by *ethically* using a random sampling method to determine from a single pool who will and who won't get subjected to or offered what you want to test? If so, you may be able to conduct an experiment! If not, move on.

Correlation

If it isn't feasible or ethical to conduct an experiment, maybe you can test for association, or correlation. You might examine association between variables in a client group, for example, such as gender and patterns of attendance, or in an employee group, such as level or type of position and use of the employee assistance program (EAP). Clearly, you can't manipulate patterns of attendance or use of the EAP, but you can try to examine them in relation to other variables for certain groups of interest. You might test association between two groups, such as the day shift and the night shift support staff, around a variable of interest, such as absenteeism. Again, you can't force absenteeism in order to study it, but as a supervisor you might be interested in association between shift and absenteeism patterns. As practitioner, program designer, or fund-raiser you might be interested in the long-term impact of a particular organizational approach to service on a variable such as recidivism rate. See the chapters on these design types for more ideas about how each one might be used for program evaluation.

OVERVIEW OF METHOD

The basic steps of program evaluation according to Smith's (1990) model are as follows:

1. You describe the program to be studied through qualitative or quantitative data or both (program statistics, interviews, questionnaires, etc.). With this you provide a context for implementation.

2. You define program goals (using formal documentation, such as mission statements, bylaws, formal program goals) to determine differences between what was intended and what is really happening. With this you provide a context for analysis.
3. You select a design:
   - Select an overall design based on your study's purpose.
   - Select a data-collection plan (any of the three major methods is appropriate).
   - Select either an entire population or a sample, depending on real numbers. In all but exploratory studies random sampling is used to show that the sample isn't biased (such as selecting people who are most positive about a program).
4. Implement the study.
5. Analyze the data.
6. Report your results to the organization.

Large-scale descriptive or other studies that collect quantitative data are often of interest to those in policy positions, program planners, and development and fund-raising personnel. Smaller studies or those that focus on collecting qualitative data are often of interest to program planners and practitioners. However, remember that they're *all* being delivered in a political climate, so be rigorous in method, be sensitive in implementation, and be aware in reporting.

MAJOR POINTS TO REMEMBER

- Program evaluation is the study of organizations with goals of professional accountability and consumer empowerment.
- Conceptualized as a research method, program evaluation provides a scientifically accepted protocol for the study process and helps to prevent biased or haphazard judgments (Smith, 1990).
- Conceptualized as practice, program evaluation provides a service by helping an organization examine its internal and external health (Smith, 1990).
- As a field of study, program evaluation assesses the quality of social policies, programs, and interventions (Smith, 1990).
- Because program evaluation is always carried out in a political environment its rigor helps to ensure that the investigator is, and is seen as, objective (Smith, 1990).

- All major designs (exploratory, descriptive, experimental, and correlational) can be considered.
- Any of the three major data-collection methods or a combination thereof can be considered.
- In all but exploratory studies random sampling is used.
- Analysis consists of whichever type is appropriate to the data-collection method used.

EXERCISE

Try It On for Size

Think about the many types of organizations, public and private, that exist in relation to your topic of interest.

1. Applying each of the four major types of design as outlined in this book, how might you carry out a piece of program evaluation in one of those organizations?
2. What internal and/or external and human or other resources would you need to carry out the study?
3. What obstacles might you encounter? How could they be overcome?
4. How might each of the four design types be applied to a study of the internal working of the organization?
5. How might they be applied to a study of the organization's service-delivery mechanisms?
6. In each case, how would you develop a sample? Would it be randomly selected? Why or why not, and what difference would it make?
7. What kinds of data-collection instruments might be appropriate?
8. Who, both inside and outside of the organization, might be interested in your findings?

REFERENCE

Smith, M. (1990). *Program Evaluation in the Human Services.* New York: Springer Publishing Company.

Chapter 14

Working Toward Reliability
(Is Your Ruler Correct?)
and Validity
(Are You Reaching the Heart of the Matter?)

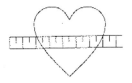

KEY CONCEPTS

accuracy
asking the right questions
clarity
consistency
integrity
knowing "it" when you see "it"
measurement
observation
operationalization
reliability
specificity
validity

INTRODUCTION

The concept of measurement is central to instrument design, and to talk about measurement is to talk about reliability and validity. These are the concepts that give your study integrity. How they pertain in particular to qualitative data is discussed more specifically in Chapter 18.

Reliability is when you use an instrument with a group of people, turn the clock back, use it again with them in exactly the same conditions, and get exactly the same results. A rubber ruler, for example, may stretch and is therefore not as reliable as a metal ruler.

Validity is when an instrument taps into (measures) what you want to tap into and nothing but that. Thus, a metal metric ruler may be reliable, but it's not a valid measure of inches.

Clearly, for a whole instrument to be reliable and valid, each item must be designed with those goals in mind. Thus, this discussion pertains to those two levels. When you think about these concepts, think of the whole instrument and each item on it.

Let's say you're interested in anger in children. You train ten people to observe children at various school playgrounds and to use the same checklist with concrete indicators of anger "in action" (operation).

What will that checklist contain? How will observers "know" anger when they see it? Those behaviors that are easiest to note over and over again by all of them (such as hitting someone or sticking out a tongue or foot stomping or crying) are the most reliable, but are they all valid indicators of anger *and nothing but* anger? Of course not. You can probably come think of several reasons other than anger for each of these examples. Designing items to be both reliable and valid is not always easy. In fact, and instruments intended to measure complex phenomena can often be a long-term (pre)occupation—field-tested over and over again and subjected to statistical tests and content analysis.

Let's say you want clients' opinions about your agency service. You might ask, "Has *X* service been useful to you?" (with *yes/no* options) or "How do you feel about *X* service?" (with *very good* to *very poor* options). If you want to know what they *think* (opinion) you need to ask exactly that. Asking about utility or feelings isn't the same as asking for opinion. And asking for feelings doesn't reach for opinions either. Picky? Yes, but for a good reason. Only by asking for exactly what you want is your question (item) valid. What do you really want to know? *That's* the first question to be asked and answered.

A BALANCING ACT: PURPOSE AND TRADE-OFFS

These two rules of thumb are useful to follow:

1. The clearer and more specific the questions and the fewer the response categories, the higher the potential for *reliability*. Thus, a *yes/no* response option is very reliable. It's highly doubtful that if you answer yes once and turn the clock back you'd then answer no to the same question *in the same circumstances*.
2. The more the questions capture the range of possibility in response (the full flavor of possibilities), the higher the potential for *validity*. Thus, although a *yes/no* response option is highly reliable, response options such as "very much in favor, somewhat in favor, neutral, somewhat against, very much against" are more likely to capture subtleties or the gray areas, where many people fit on many issues.

Since these two rules seem to contradict each other, can you achieve both? You can certainly work toward both and achieve a high level of each. Often, however, the issue is one of trade-offs, and how you lean depends on the purpose of your study. What do you really want or need to know? What amount of detail is necessary? For each item ask yourself:

1. What information, *exactly,* am I going to get by designing it in this particular way?
2. Is that enough, or do I want more detail—even perhaps something slightly different from what this item phrased in this way will get me?

For example, each of these five questions asks for something slightly different:

How do you feel about our program?
What do you like about our program?

What do you like best about our program?
What is most useful about our program?
What do you think of our program?

Given the complexities of the human condition, social science measures never achieve 100 percent reliability and validity. It's simply too difficult to develop consensus on operational definitions across generations and cultures. Without too much trouble we might develop a number of indicators that, when combined, provide a fairly reliable and valid overall measure of anger in children, for example. It's far more challenging to develop reliable and valid indicators for such concepts as religiosity, bigotry, apathy, health, illness, etc. The more you study concrete behavior, then, the easier to design highly reliable and valid instruments.

Furthermore, theories of human nature change. Just twenty years ago we routinely asked people their race without qualm, but today we struggle to distinguish between race, ethnicity, and even culture. We once asked about sexual preference but today distinguish between sex and gender, identity and orientation, and self-image and behavior. In short, what we think we know changes constantly. Is church-going a valid indicator of spirituality? It's certainly a reliable one; we'd all recognize churchgoing behavior if we saw it. Is it truly a sign of spirituality? That's not so clear.

WORKING TOWARD RELIABILITY: THE RUBBER RULER PITFALL

To work toward reliability is to work out the technical kinks in an instrument, which can be done in several ways. You don't necessarily carry out all of them; the ones you choose make sense with your study's purpose and design.

1. Be very clear and specific in designing each item/question on the instrument and in the instructions.
2. Administer the same instrument twice to the same people and compare results *(test/retest)*. The more similar they are, the more reliable the instrument.
3. Design two instruments *(parallel forms)* to measure one variable (e.g., bigotry). Give both to the same people, and compare results. If Mr. X reveals himself a bigot on both instruments, both tests are reliable.

4. If your instrument is large (e.g., 100 items) with duplicate items, split it into two equal halves, each containing items that go after the same data (*split-half* test). Carry out a parallel forms test. The two halves can be assessed for equality through a *coefficient alpha* statistical test.

5. Do everything possible to keep testing conditions equal for you and/or assistants (*interrater/interobserver* reliability). Don't observe or interview some when you're alert and others when you're exhausted, for example.

6. Do everything possible to keep testing conditions equal for participants (*respondent* reliability). Don't conduct some interviews in a private space and others in a public space, or some when the respondents have time and others when they're in a hurry, for example.

WORKING TOWARD VALIDITY: REACHING THE HEART OF THE MATTER

Four types of validity must be considered. However, you don't normally select one over the other. Again, the purpose of your study logically dictates which to consider most, although all instruments are expected to work toward *construct* validity (you'll see why later in this section). Review the purpose of your study, and reread your question or hypothesis. Then ask yourself the following questions:

1. *Am I interested in this instrument to predict the future of whoever responds to it?* If so, you're interested in *predictive validity.* Measures such as the GREs and SATs are designed with this ability in mind.

   What do you do? You administer the instrument and wait to see what happens to the respondents in the future. If you get a positive correlation between their earlier scores on your instrument and future performance, the instrument can be said to have predictive validity. This kind of testing takes years.

2. *Am I interested in measuring differences among respondents now?* If so, you're interested in *concurrent validity;* you want to see how people vary in the present (as in knowledge, skill, atti-

tude, etc.). What do you do? You use two different and feasible data-collection methods to study the same thing *(triangulation),* such as observation and interviews.

Suppose you want to study the way practitioners deal with conflict in client groups. In the interviews they describe their interventions, but how do you know they really operate that way? You don't. However, if you then observe them in action you can judge for yourself. If both the interview and observation indicate the same conflict resolution methods are used, then both your interview guide and the checklist used for observation purposes have good concurrent validity. In other words, they each ask the right questions and get the real "scoop." If discrepancies exist, you need to rethink the instruments and data-collection methods.

3. *Am I interested in using this instrument to measure (tap into/study) complex concepts?* If so, you're interested in *construct validity;* most instruments intended to study complex phenomena are designed to work toward this type of validity.

As noted, with a bit of work we could develop an observation checklist of indicators for apathy, for example, and then "know" it when we "see" it. To do so for its more complex social form, anomie, however, would be more difficult. Imagine the challenge of sending ten assistants not only to seek out anomic social systems but then to agree on anomie when they think they see it! Social science research is often interested in precisely these issues.

The dilemma is how to measure complex constructs when scientific standards require precise operational definitions (indicators). The answer is to anchor your indicators in a theoretical base (which you do by reviewing the literature). Anchoring your work in theory gives your study its greatest credibility and validity.

4. *Finally, can I achieve content validity? Content validity* refers to the logic of your instrument "on the face of it"—if it at least seems to measure what you want. Often exploratory studies go into such new territory that there is no theoretical body of knowledge for anchoring question; therefore, construct validity is impossible to achieve. In that case, you solicit expert feed-

back about the nature and design of your questions or items, *on the face of it.*

In a nutshell, then, to work toward reliability and validity of a research instrument means to work out both technical and conceptual kinks.

MAJOR POINTS TO REMEMBER

- Measurement speaks to reliability and validity of instruments used to study something.
- Two rules of thumb: The clearer, more specific the questions and fewer the response categories, the higher the potential to achieve reliability; the subtler, the higher the potential to achieve validity.
- To work toward reliability is to fix technical flaws.
- To work toward validity is to fix conceptual flaws.
- It is difficult for social science measures to achieve 100 percent reliability and validity.

EXERCISE

Ask Yourself

Write down some closed-ended questions/items that you might include on an instrument to study your topic of interest along with their response options (true/false, multiple choice, etc.). Now for each one ask yourself the following questions and undertake the subsequent steps:

1. Is it phrased as clearly as possible? Enough words? Too many words? The right words? Is it brief but concise?
2. Is it really asking the question I want answered?
3. Is the response option designed as clearly as possible?
4. Show your questions to others for feedback.
5. Rework your questions/items.
6. For each item repeat numbers 2 through 5.

It's time-consuming but well worth your effort!

Chapter 15

Sampling

(Going to the Source)

KEY CONCEPTS

generalization
implications
nonrandom samples
probability
random samples
randomization
populations
sample frames

INTRODUCTION

Sample (v): to select elements (people, cases, objects) that conform to the criteria needed in order to participate in your study.

Sample (n): the group of elements (people, cases, objects) that participates in your study.

A sample represents a portion of a *population* of interest to you (i.e., the total number of elements [people, cases, objects] that conform to some designated criteria). A population might be large or small, and how that population is defined can vary from study to study. All social workers holding a master of social work (MSW) degree in the United States might be a population of interest; all MSW social workers in New York State might be the population; all MSW social workers in New York City might be the population of interest; all MSW social workers in the New York City Administration for Children's Services might be the population; all MSW social workers in a private organization who belong to the National Association of Social Workers (NASW) might be the population. You can imagine that the size of each of these populations varies tremendously in spite of their convergence on "MSW social workers."

If every element (people, cases, objects) of a population is identical in every way, we don't need to obtain samples; we simply study each one or the most handy, depending on size. That's rarely the case, however, except in certain program evaluation studies that may have access to all employees, for example, or all clients. In general, we use one of several possible sampling methods to develop a manageable group to study.

GOING TO THE SOURCE

Your goal is to access the sources that will best give you the information you want. The group composed of those sources is called your sample. Samples are said to be either *probability* or *nonprobability* samples.

PROBABILITY SAMPLES: FORMS AND METHODS

Probability samples are called such because the elements from your population of interest that end up in your sample are dictated by probability theory (chance). They're obtained through one of four possible *random-sampling* methods. In research lingo *random* does not mean haphazard; it means that sample selection is dictated by probability, not by you.

It's appropriate to use a probability-sampling method when (1) you can specify for each element its probability of being included in the sample and (2) each element has an equal chance of being included in that sample. Every person in a population of 100 has an equal and known (1 percent) chance of being included in a final sample of ten for example.

Probability samples are usually associated with descriptive, experimental, and correlational designs. The goal of working with a probability sample is to generalize your findings to the sample's larger population. You study a small portion of a population because to study it in its entirety is unwieldy. Your ultimate interest is in the population as a whole, however. Thus, by keeping your fingers out of the process of who gets to participate and so reducing the potential for sample bias, probability samples permit generalization.

There are four types of probability samples: simple random, systematic random, stratified random, and cluster. The one you select depends on feasibility, purpose of study, and how much control you're willing to surrender over who or what ends up in your sample. You'll see differences exists, even within the "family" of probability methods.

Simple Random Sample

This is the classic, best-known type of sample and the most reliable for making generalizations, because who or what ends up in it is the most completely dictated by probability (i.e., the least interfered with by human hands) or, said conversely, is the least likely to be biased. It's often likened to picking numbers out of a hat.

Overview of Method

1. Identify your *population of interest* (such as MSW social workers in New York City who are members of NASW).
2. Obtain a *sampling frame,* i.e., a roster of all the elements in that population (such as a current roster of NYC NASW members).
3. Assign each element a number beginning with no. 1. (Thus, the first name becomes #1, the second #2, the third #3, etc.)
4. Decide on *sample size* (e.g., out of a sampling frame of 1,000 a final sample of 100). There are no rules around size, but thirty elements is generally the minimum for statistical analysis. The bigger the better, as long at it doesn't become cumbersome.

5. Use a *table of random numbers* (in every research or stats book or many computer statistical programs) to select the 100 elements for your final sample. How? The first 100 four-digit numbers (in order to give number 1,000 a chance too) you come to in a table of random numbers that match the numbers of your elements or identified by the computer program become your sample.

Strengths and Weaknesses

This sample type offers the greatest potential for generalization because of all the methods, sample membership is most dictated by probability theory and thus least potentially biased. However, it can be unwieldy to use with huge numbers. Even with a computer program to identify random numbers, you may need to assign the initial number to every element in the sampling frame by hand. The next method is often used as a good alternative.

Systematic Random Sample

This method is less complicated, because you don't need to assign a number to each element or use a table of random numbers.

Overview of Method

1. Identify your *population of interest* (such as MSW social workers in New York City who are members of NASW).
2. Obtain a *sampling frame*, i.e., a roster of all the elements in that population (such as a current roster of NYC NASW members).
3. Decide on *sample size* (e.g., out of a sampling frame of 1,000 a final sample of 100). Again, thirty elements is generally the minimum for statistical analysis, and the bigger the better, as long at it doesn't become unwieldy.
4. Develop your sample by selecting every nth element on the sampling frame until you have enough (100). To know what "every nth element" is you divide the sampling frame total (1,000) by your final sample (100). Here, then, the "nth" interval is ten, so you'd select every tenth element to end finish with 100.
5. Pick the first anywhere before your first "nth" (here, it's ten) by using a table of random numbers (or throwing dice or picking a

number out of a hat, etc.). The number you get is your first sample member; the others are at every nth interval thereafter.

Strengths and Weaknesses

This method is easier to use than simple random. Its major disadvantage is the possibility that some unknown order is operating on your sampling frame and introducing a bias. If the sampling frame is cyclical in a way that coincides with your nth interval (e.g., it has a five-element cycle but you don't know it, and you're choosing every fifth element), it's possible that you'll draw a grossly biased sample.

Stratified Random Sample

This sample is developed to ensure that desired categories of elements are represented. Thus, it combines some reliance on probability theory with some control by you, because you don't completely trust chance to give you good representation through either simple or systematic methods. For example, in a population in which a vast majority of people are female, you might worry that males will be underrepresented.

Overview of Method

1. Identify your *population of interest* (such as MSW social workers in New York City who are members of NASW).
2. Obtain a *sampling frame*, i.e., a roster of all the elements in that population (such as a current roster of NYC NASW members).
3. Decide on *sample size* (e.g., out of a sampling frame of 1,000 a final sample of 100). No rules around size, but as stated, thirty elements is generally the minimum for statistical analysis, and the bigger the better, unless unmanageable.
4. Divide sampling frame into *strata* that are mutually exclusive on a variable that you want particularly represented. Let's say it's age group for your study. You then develop stratum one for persons under forty, stratum two for persons from forty-one to sixty, and stratum three for persons over sixty.
5. *Simple or systematic sample each stratum*—for example, thirty-three cases from one, thirty-three from two, thirty-four from three. If one stratum is much larger than the other(s), you can

pick proportionately to have more of one and less of another. Often, for example, strata of females are larger than those of males. Thus, you might decide to obtain sixty-five subjects from a female stratum and thirty-five from a male stratum. This is called *weighting*.

6. Combine the elements from each stratum into a final sample.

Strengths and Weaknesses

This method ensures representation along certain variables, particularly when the sampling frame may include gross differences—often the case for race or gender or age group, for example. By increasing your control, however (by not letting probability theory completely dictate the sample), you also increase the potential for bias.

Cluster

Much social science research involves the study of megapopulations for which it's difficult to obtain sampling frames, such as the residents of a very large city or for large categories, such as all college students in the United States or all Florida churchgoers. In these cases, cluster sampling is an option. Cluster sampling typically involves two sampling levels: an initial sampling of groups or "clusters" followed by a secondary sampling of individual elements (e.g., persons).

Overview of Method

1. Identify your *population of interest* (e.g., all churchgoers in Florida).
2. Obtain an *initial sampling frame* of groups or "clusters," in this case a list of discrete churches in that state.
3. Decide on an *initial sample size*. Let's say there are 5,000 discrete churches in Florida. They're your initial sampling frame. Let's say you decide on 500 churches.
4. From the list of 5,000 churches, you use simple, systematic, or stratified random sampling to select the initial sample (500 churches).

5. You then obtain a *secondary sampling frame,* in this case lists from the 500 churches of their individual members. These lists of individual members are your secondary sampling frame.
6. Let's say the 500 lists contain 20,000 names. You then use simple, systematic, or stratified random sampling to select the *final sample* (say 2,000 individuals).
7. You can add more levels (such as sampling a city for zoning areas, sampling zoning areas for blocks, and sampling the blocks for households, etc.) until you pare down to the actual unit you want to study.

Strengths and Weaknesses

Cluster sampling makes it possible to study large and unruly things by breaking them down into more manageable elements. Although it's very efficient because it moves you from the cosmic to the workable, you do increase the potential for sample bias. Every time you carry out a probability-sampling process, it is said to be subject to one sample error (a way of acknowledging the inevitable humanity factor in all we do). Thus, with one level of sampling you're already subject to one sampling error; with cluster sampling, you become subject to at least two sampling errors and possibly more if you add more levels.

Recap of Basic Advantages of Probability Samples

In sum, the basic advantages to probability sampling are as follows:
1. It helps to rule out human biases that might be involved in more casual selection.
2. It enhances the likelihood of accurate representation by letting probability (chance) determine your sample.
3. Its reliance on probability theory lets you estimate the degree of error you can expect with your sample. The smaller the error, the better.

A note of caution: If you end up with a sample quite different from your original one (because, for example, some people never returned your questionnaire or dropped out of a program you're testing or become unavailable for further observation), your ability to generalize diminishes.

NONPROBABILITY SAMPLES: FORMS AND METHODS

Nonprobability samples are obtained through one of three possible *nonrandom sampling* methods. It's appropriate to use nonrandom methods when (1) there's no way to estimate the probability of inclusion for any one element or (2) you can't make sure they all have an equal chance of being included in the first place.

Nonrandom sampling is usually associated with exploratory design because when little is known about a subject, you aren't picky about getting the information, and your methodological priority becomes getting at that information. The ultimate goal of working with a nonprobability sample is to develop implications for action or further thought and study, although each of the three methods takes a slightly different approach to exploration.

Size of sample is less of an issue in nonprobability forms than for probability forms, which are intended to permit generalization. Whereas the rule of thumb for probability samples is a minimum of thirty cases, (although that's not always possible in some experimental designs, for example), the rule of thumb for nonprobability samples is that there must be some logic between the research question and consideration of sample size and that data yield must be rich in quality. Some studies explore single cases, while studies that seek variety in perspective (e.g., the viewpoints of upper and middle management, line workers, and support staff) need larger numbers.

Accidental

This sample is simply the cases at hand, whoever or whatever is easily available, such as the first ten people to walk in the room or to pass through the train station or who are willing to answer you (e.g., a "man on the street" approach).

Overview of Method

1. Identify the best (i.e., efficient, effective) *context* for having the right cases at hand to answer your research question.
2. Decide on *sample size.*

3. Develop a *data-collection plan* (i.e., how and when to go to the site and how to get the information you need; see Chapter 16).
4. Carry out a *pilot test* (i.e., enter the context to assess the likelihood of its yielding both the quality and quantity of data you seek).
5. Implement the study.

Strengths and Weaknesses

This method allows us to study groups and phenomena that might not be otherwise available or accessible. Its primary weakness is its potential for sample bias, although that is to some extent a moot issue because generalization is not a priority. Researcher bias is, of course, an issue to consider, manage, and counteract through careful self-analysis.

Quota

Similar to stratified random sampling, quota sampling identifies desired characteristics and then ensures that cases with those characteristics are included in the sample. In contrast, however, elements are selected purposely. That is, you don't use any random sampling but just go after cases with that characteristic until it's "well enough" represented. Are you concerned that persons with an income below the poverty line be represented in your sample? Then make sure you go after what you consider to be "enough" such participants.

Overview of Method

1. Identify which participant/case *characteristics are crucial* to your sample.
2. Decide on *sample size.*
3. Develop a *data-collection plan* (i.e., how you're going to get the information you need/see Chapter 16).
4. Identify and get the information desired from cases that will yield good *representation* around the characteristics identified.

Strengths and Weaknesses

This method ensures representation along certain variables of importance. It's not fruitful to recruit a very small sample this way, however, because the smaller it is the less heterogeneity has real meaning.

For example, it's less reasonable to draw inferences about gender in a sample of ten with five men and five women than in one of thirty with fifteen men and fifteen women. This method also has the potential to be grossly biased, making it important to consider and report all aspects of context, such as geographic location or age range or perhaps racial or religious or cultural composition of the sample, etc. As with all nonprobability methods, however, it can identify variables, create implications, and provide valuable food for further thought and study.

Purposive

This sample consists of purposely selected elements (people, cases, objects) because of their particular characteristics, either (1) extreme, such as known experts or pioneers in a field, or (2) typical, such as people with a certain illness or social situation of interest. Quota samples are also purposive to the extent that you select "enough" cases with certain characteristics, but purposive samples are drawn from an available population without stratifying first.

For example, you might seek out expert researchers to help you formulate your research problem or gain theoretical insights or identify potentially important concepts. In these cases you would purposely locate them for their ability to help you rather than because of their gender or age range, etc. You might also seek out practitioners who are expert at working with certain groups or problems. In some cases, those experts also may be "typical." For example, practitioners are experts about their approach to practice, but they also reflect typical cases of persons whose behavior you want to study.

Overview of Method

1. Identify the *best sources* for obtaining the information needed to answer your research question (either experts or typical cases).
2. Decide on *sample size*.
3. Develop a *data-collection plan* (i.e., how you're going to get the information you need/see Chapter 16).

Strengths and Weaknesses

This method ensures representation either in expertise or object, increasing your ability to get your questions answered. Here, bias is a good thing because you *want* sample members to be extreme (expert) or you *want* them to be typical objects of interest. In other words, you *want* your sample to be biased in a certain direction. Once again, its weakness is that, similar to other nonprobability methods, it doesn't permit generalization. Your findings must remain contextual, i.e., about the sample itself. Remember, however, that generalization is not its ultimate goal.

Recap of Basic Advantages of Nonprobability Samples

In sum, the major reasons for using nonprobability sampling methods are as follows:

1. they're convenient;
2. you can make choices of inclusion/exclusion and don't have to use a complex randomization or computerization process;
3. they're efficient, generally needing less time and money than a random selection process; and
4. they make it easier to access populations that would otherwise be difficult to reach and for which it would be even more difficult to develop a sampling frame, such as homeless persons in a large city or underground cultures.

MAJOR POINTS TO REMEMBER

- To sample is to select elements (people, cases, objects) to participate in your study.
- A sample is a group of elements that participates in your study.
- A sample is a piece of a population of interest (total number of elements) that conform to some criteria, such as age range, gender, geographic location, professional degree, etc.
- Probability theory dictates membership in probability samples.
- You dictate membership in nonprobability samples.
- A probability sample, obtained through one of four possible random-sampling methods, is appropriate when you can specify for each element its chance of being included and when each element has an equal chance of being included.
- A nonprobability sample, obtained through one of three possible nonrandom-sampling methods, is appropriate when you cannot estimate the probability of inclusion for any element or can't make sure they all have an equal chance of inclusion.

- The ultimate goal of using a probability sample is generalization, whereas the ultimate goal of using a nonprobability sample is to have access to information in the first place.
- Probability samples are usually associated with descriptive, experimental, and correlational studies. Nonprobability samples are generally associated with exploratory studies.
- The purpose of your study suggests a sampling method, although real-world factors, such as cost, inability to get a sampling frame, etc., can require rethinking and redirection.

EXERCISE

Sample a Sample

So, you have a research problem stated in sentence form that's clear enough to repeat nonchalantly when people ask about it? You've also got the design down pat (sort of)? Now you need a source of information? Ask yourself the following:

1. Does a probability sample make sense for this study? Why or why not?
2. Does a nonprobability sample make sense for this study? Why or why not?
3. If a probability sample, which of the following four makes most sense and why?
- Simple random
- Systematic random
- Stratified random
- Cluster
4. Would your choice be feasible? If so, how would the selection process actually look? If not, then what? What are other realistic options?
5. If a nonprobability sample, which of the following three makes most sense and why?
- Accidental
- Quota
- Purposive
6. Would your choice be feasible? If so, how would the selection process actually look? If not, then what? What are other realistic options?

Chapter 16
Data Collection
(Getting to the Answers)

KEY CONCEPTS

interview
objectivity
observation
person-in-situation
questionnaire
reliability
self-report
specificity
structure
subjectivity
validity

INTRODUCTION

There are three major data-collection methods: observation, interviews, and questionnaires. Each one has several possible variations, and studies often combine methods. The methods are presented here in terms of advantages and disadvantages. Your selection depends theoretically on the purpose of your study and in real-world terms on such factors as access, expense, etc.

In each case it's important to consider the vulnerability of the population you're studying. The more vulnerable it is, the less you should assume that a signed informed consent form truly reflects consent.

Many factors may compel people to accommodate your request, including a sense of power differential and the desire to avoid negative repercussions that may accompany a decline. Thus, interviewing colleagues, for example, is one thing; interviewing people we call clients is another.

OBSERVATION

Advantages

- You can "see" things for yourself.
- You can see behaviors in their natural settings.
- You don't have to rely on self-reporting.
- You don't usually need to prepare much material.
- You can use this method with all populations regardless of their literary or verbal skills.
- You don't need to rely on willingness to participate.

Disadvantages

- High potential for subjective interpretation on the part of the observer(s).
- High potential for rater/interrater bias.
- Your presence may contaminate the setting or situation and result in questionable validity of whatever is being observed.
- You can observe only the "here and now" and only draw inferences about the past or future.
- Observation can be time-consuming and expensive.

Issues to Consider

1. Because there's a high potential for subjective interpretation, observers must be well trained to keep that kind of bias to a minimum. Also, the high potential for rater and interrater bias may make it difficult to evaluate and/or code the results.
2. You may control a bit for the potential that your presence contaminates the setting and thus increase the validity of what's being observed. For example, you might spend time in the obser-

vation context to get people accustomed to seeing you in hopes that whatever behavioral changes might still occur because of your initial presence will eventually diminish.

3. Sometimes it seems as if informed consent for observation will interfere with the purpose of the study (that there's a need to see behavior in authentic vivo, for example, or that high-status or powerful people may not want to be observed), causing tension between the ethics of informed consent and need for information. Even if other fields argue in favor of "need to know," however, professional values of individual autonomy and self-determination take some precedence in social work research. See the NASW Code of Ethics as a guide.

INTERVIEW

Advantages

- You control the process to get exactly the information you want.
- You can address complex issues.
- You can clarify questions and responses.
- You can make both the format (how you do what you do) and process (what you do) as rigid or flexible as you wish.
- You can observe the "person in situation."
- You can use it with illiterate persons.
- You have access to nonverbal cues.
- It is easier to get people's cooperation for interviews than for written narratives outside of your presence.
- You have a high response rate because you control the process.

Disadvantages

- Your presence may affect (i.e., bias) the situation or the setting (such as eliciting socially desirable responses).
- Your personality may affect (i.e., bias) the situation.
- The quality of your interaction may have unwanted effects on responses.
- Conducting interviews can be expensive and time consuming.

Issues to Consider

1. How can you know when the interview is over, other than the fact that the clock is running out? When you think the person has "said it all," ask for a bit more. When he or she starts repeating himself or herself, you're probably done.
2. Your personality, the quality of your interaction, and even your mere presence may bias the process, so maintain as neutral a presence as possible. This doesn't mean being aloof; it means appearing cordial, even friendly, and without judgment as you ask questions and hear answers. The only facial expression you should don is one that shows interest and attention. Use your practice skills.
3. Don't hit and run! Give people a chance to brief and to debrief. A few moments to make sure the person is prepared for the interview and a few moments to talk freely afterward will benefit both of you. You can also use debriefing time to ask about the possibility of a feedback session, when you can take your analysis and interpretations back for confirmation.
4. Be polite. The respondent is helping you, regardless of your subject. Don't take an aggressive mind-set, even if you're asking about issues on which your opinions, attitudes, or feelings are different from those of the interviewee. It's only because he or she is willing to talk with you that you've got a study going, no matter what you think of the responses! If you do feel aggressive, let someone else do the interviews, or choose another method.
5. Finally, if you're asking people to talk about subjects that require deep thought, consider sending them a copy of your interview guide ahead of time. Remember, your purpose isn't to meet with them and "trick" a quick, off-the-cuff response. It's to get thoughtful and considered narrative material in response to your questions.

QUESTIONNAIRE

Advantages

- Questionnaires can be highly reliable.
- Questionnaires have the potential for a high degree of validity if they allow respondents time and privacy to think through their responses.
- Because they are standardized, questionnaires are usually easy to analyze.
- Questionnaires allow study of the past and future as well as the "here and now."
- Questionnaires are relatively inexpensive and easy to administer to large numbers and/or over a wide geographic area.

Disadvantages

- Highly structured questionnaires may force people into categories that do not accurately reflect them.
- Questionnaires do not allow clarification, expansion, or explanation by either researcher or respondent.
- Questionnaires require some degree of literacy.
- People must be able to express themselves in writing.
- There's no opportunity to observe nonverbal communication.

Issues to Consider

1. Designing a questionnaire that's both highly reliable and captures the full flavor of respondents' positions (valid) isn't an easy task, so if you're not using one already available, consider the time it will take to design it, field test (pilot test) it, and rework it until it's both reliable and valid. Don't do this alone. Get feedback on the design and testing process from others in the know.
2. Remember that highly structured questionnaires don't allow either you or the respondent any opportunity to clarify or expand on questions or answers (either in writing, verbally, or nonverbally), so design your items with that in mind.

3. Because questionnaires have such a low return rate, be sure to distribute many more than you need as a final sample.
4. Regardless of method, find a way to send participants a thank-you note! It may have to be "up front" with questionnaires, as in the introduction/invitation cover letter.

MAJOR POINTS TO REMEMBER

- The three major data-collection methods are observation, interviews, and questionnaires.
- Each method has possible variations, and studies often combine them.
- Which method to select depends in theory on the purpose of your study and in real-world terms on feasibility.

EXERCISE

From Theory to the Real World

Data collection is where theory meets the real world—where you determine exactly how you're going to do what you need to do to get your answers. As you begin this process, ask yourself the following:

1. As exactly as possible, what information do I need to best answer my research question as it's formulated?
2. What setting/situation/context is going to be most conducive to my getting the information I'm after? Do I need to observe behavior? Am I looking for a fringe or invisible or underground population? Do I want people to sit and talk with me? Am I more likely to get the information I need through anonymity? Where and how might I find the sample I'm interested in to obtain the information I need?

   Whichever data-collection method you've chosen, even if it's tentative, think about the purpose of your study and ask yourself:

- Does this method make the most sense? Why or why not? (Consider political and strategic issues, costs, access, privacy factors, ethics, etc.)
- To what extent will this method influence my findings? Will they be so idiosyncratic that they won't present much food for thought for other contexts? If so, will that be okay? Why or why not? If not, then what?
- Should I get the information I need from people who are the objects of my study or from others? In either case, why or why not?

3. Should I be the (only) one to collect data? Why or why not? What impact will I (or assistants) have on the method I have in mind? (This might range from very low [e.g., *Well, you could say that my worldview or general perspective is what made me choose this subject*] to very high [e.g., *I think my presence would have a great impact because I'll be very visible as an observer*]).

4. Would that impact be acceptable given the purpose of my study? Why or why not? If not, then what?

Chapter 17

Data Analysis: An Overview

(Okay, You've Got the Answers . . . *Now* What?)

KEY CONCEPTS

constructivism
content analysis
meaning
logical positivism
qualitative
quantitative
significance

INTRODUCTION

To analyze data is to make meaning of your results, both descriptively (what they are) and interpretively (what they indicate, suggest, imply, etc.). It is to complete a kind of puzzle that, when finished, tells a story.

QUALITATIVE DATA ANALYSIS

Qualitative data refers to material collected in the form of written words. Qualitative data analysis, usually associated with exploratory studies, consists of content analysis, i.e., analyzing the written word, sometimes called narratives.

To carry out qualitative analysis is to do much work during and after implementation in the form of content analysis as each narrative is transcribed and analyzed, so expect and save that time! Analysis, description, and interpretation of qualitative data all revolve around the purpose of your study, which provides the context for making meaning of the data and usually to the end of theory building—some overall story about your sample.

Two primary sources for organizing qualitative data are (1) the questions on the interview guide and (2) the insights that emerge as you collect and/or analyze the data. It's acceptable to begin with either one, and it's fine to change your mind along the way; in fact, it would be crazy *not* to change your organizing framework if the one you're using begins to make less sense while another one takes shape! The name of the game is *flexibility.*

QUANTITATIVE DATA ANALYSIS

The term *Quantitative data* (*data* is plural, by the way) refers to material collected in actual numerical form (such as number of years) or to which we've assigned numerical codes (such as multiple-choice codes).

Quantitative data analysis, usually associated with large-scale descriptive studies, experiments, and correlational studies, consists of understanding numbers (statistics) in two ways: (1) as they describe your findings (how people responded) and (2) as they help you to infer the significance (degree of reality/truth/accuracy) of your findings for the sample itself and the extent to which you can confidently generalize those findings to the population from which you drew your sample.

Statistics

Statistics are simply numbers that help us make meaning of quantitative data. Descriptive stats give a summary look at sample characteristics and responses. Inferential stats, which are based on descriptive stats, help us determine the significance of our quantitative findings.

To carry out quantitative analysis is to spend much time designing or choosing an appropriate standardized instrument (so, front-heavy labor), with a fairly easy go of it later on, when analysis consists of examining and interpreting numbers. To make meaning of quantitative data is using statistics to summarize, organize, describe, and interpret your findings.

Using Descriptive Statistics

Descriptive stats summarize your data in visual nutshells through tables, charts, and graphs. Some visuals offer a blow-by-blow description of each item/question (variable), called *univariate* analysis (gender, age, religious affiliation, number of siblings, number of years in practice, etc.). Some describe if (how) two items/questions (variables) relate to each other in your sample, called *bivariate* analysis (e.g., how each gender as a group responded to the question on religious affiliation, etc.). Some describe if (how) three or more items/questions (variables) relate to one another, called *multivariate* analysis (gender by age range by religious affiliation).

Using Inferential Statistics

Based on various laws of probability, *inferential stats* tell you how confidently you can *infer* that your quantitative findings are probably a real/true/accurate reflection of your sample (not due to chance or error), and how confidently you can *infer* a resemblance between your sample and the population from which you drew it. Why all this need for inference? Because after data collection you have numbers (stats) only for your sample, not for everyone the sample is supposed to represent.

Now you need to use what you know about the smaller group (sample) to learn about the larger group (population). You decided to learn about a large group by studying a small piece of it, so now you must back your way into knowing that larger group, so to speak, through inference. That's what inferential stats do; based on your sample's descriptive stats, they help you determine if your sample findings "hold water" for the larger group as well.

Inferential stats come from various mathematical formulas called *tests of statistical significance,* which are based on your descriptive stats. They're selected according to the level of measure (LOM) of the variable(s) in question and whether you're looking at difference or association. They result in certain numbers (stats), each of which tells you something about your potential for inference.

THE GREAT DEBATE: QUALITATIVE VERSUS QUANTITATIVE

For years on end people have argued over the scientific legitimacy of qualitative data on one hand and the practical utility or even validity of quantitative data on the other. The heart of the argument for quantitative data is that nothing short of replicating so-called hard-science principles (rationality, objectivity, etc.) and methods (including quantification of all variables, often referred to as "hard" data) is acceptable. The proponents of this approach are referred to as *logical positivists:* their tickets to knowledge are objectivity and quantification.

The opposing camp has argued that the fluidity of human nature makes studying it through only quantitative means impossible, and that in attempting to understand the human condition, subjectivity plays just as important a role in the world (perhaps even a greater one) as so-called objectivity. The proponents of this approach are referred to as *constructivists:* their ticket to knowledge is understanding the meanings that people attach to their world.

What a waste of breath! Clearly, there's need and room for both. To debate what is "real" science is to misdirect attention to status instead of substance. Good quantitative studies offer what qualitative data cannot, and vice versa. Well-rounded pictures of anything always include many aspects or angles. Census reports offer interesting numbers about who's doing what where, and stories of tradition and culture, for example, offer interesting food for thought about who's doing what to whom, where, and *why.* Don't waste your breath on this debate!

MAJOR POINTS TO REMEMBER

- To analyze data is to make meaning of results, both descriptively and interpretively.
- Analysis consists of univariate, bivariate, and multivariate analysis.
- Qualitative data analysis is usually associated with exploratory studies and consists of analyzing the written word.
- Quantitative data analysis is usually associated with large-scale descriptive or experimental or correlational studies and consists of understanding numbers that describe your findings or those that tell you about the capacity to generalize.
- To carry out qualitative analysis is to expect a great deal of work during and after implementation.
- To carry out quantitative analysis is to spend much time in designing or choosing an appropriate standardized instrument, meaning front-heavy labor.
- Analysis, description, and interpretation of qualitative data all revolve around the purpose of a study, which provides the context for making meaning, usually to the end of theory building.
- To make meaning of quantitative data is to use numbers to summarize, organize, describe, and interpret your findings.
- Both qualitative and quantitative data have value in social work research.

EXERCISE

Get Directions

By now some study should be taking shape. What direction seems to make sense to you?

1. Does it look like an exploratory study?
   If so, then you're probably most interested in some kind of
   _____random/nonrandom) sampling, right?
   And in collecting primarily _____ (qualitative/
   quantitative) data, right?

And in carrying out _____(content/statistical) analysis, right?

2. Does it look like a descriptive study?

If so, then you're probably most interested in some kind of _____ (random/nonrandom) sampling, right?

And in collecting primarily_____(qualitative/ quantitative) data, right?

And in carrying out _____(content/statistical) analysis, right?

3. Does it look like an experiment?

If so, then you're probably most interested in some kind of _____(random/nonrandom) sampling, right?

And in collecting primarily_____(qualitative/ quantitative) data, right?

And in carrying out _____(content/statistical) analysis, right?

4. Does it look like a correlation design of some type?

If so, then you're probably most interested in some kind of _____(random/nonrandom) sampling, right?

And in collecting primarily_____(qualitative/ quantitative) data, right?

And in carrying out _____ (content/statistical) analysis, right?

5. Perhaps you'd prefer to evaluate your practice?

If so, kudos to you! How will you get your sample ($N = 1$)? What kind of _____(qualitative/quantitative) data will you collect and why? So you'll carry out some kind of _____(content/statistical) data analysis, right?

Chapter 18

Qualitative Data Analysis: Making Sense of Words

(*How* Many Pages to Look At?)

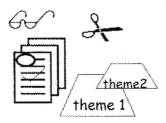

KEY CONCEPTS

audience
bias
coding
completeness
confirmability
content analysis
context
evidence
grounded theory
qualitative data
saturation
self-reflection
thick description
transferability
truth
utility

INTRODUCTION

Qualitative analysis, or analysis of words, is referred to as *content* analysis, and its basic task is to understand, interpret, and represent the meaning of what has been said. Perhaps most crucial to this process is the researcher's awareness of personal bias, ranging from those that direct him or her toward a certain topic in the first place to those that tend to hide in the back of his or her mind as analysis takes place.

Analysis begins by developing clarity about the narrative itself— by understanding the words as said. (Actually, it begins with a feeling for the flavor of their context as the environment and nonverbal cues are assessed if they result from interviews, and as field notes or memos written afterward as records of that assessment are also analyzed). It continues with some assessment of their greater meaning— the larger stories they tell.

Developing those stories is the interpretive piece of content analysis. Some stories are rather straightforward, but often they're obscure and require some artistic "reading between the lines" or extrapolation, which is why the concept of *evidence,* which refers to the narrator's own words, is central to content analysis.

Here's an important rule as you begin analysis, then: each time you move from description of what has been said to interpretation, provide solid evidence (direct quotes) as support.

Mind-Set: The Truth About Truth

People new to qualitative analysis often worry that respondents may not tell the "truth." Well, what constitutes "truth" is a long and honorable question, and when you go after people's stories you do, in fact, get their perspectives of what constitutes the "truth."

Reaching for truth in a common sense way in analysis is important, of course, but truth is always in the eyes of the storyteller when you're reaching for narrative material. That's not a bad thing; in fact, that's what you're after. You're after people's stories—how they see or saw things. They are the rightful authors of those stories. Better to focus your energy on *your* ability to interpret and represent those stories accurately. In fact, your ability to be a "truthful" reporter is probably in greater question than that of your participants. Think for a moment. Researchers (funded in one way or another) probably have more reasons than anyone else to slant their findings, no?

Since truth and perspective are often matters of degree, then, focus on your own ability to tell the truth. Be prepared to provide in writing a "thick description" of everything you did, who you did it to, and why you did it that way. Others will judge the credibility (truth) of your interpretations and applicability of your findings. Describe your methods (including all process details and obstacles), nature and characteristics of your sample (including how and why you selected it and why it is the size it is), and how you analyzed your data and why you did it that way. (Anticipate significant page space!) In fact, assume that your notes will be seen by others (someone who wishes to analyze your methods, for example), and think *utility*. Work hard to make your findings apply to the real world—in real situations with real problems.

Whoa! You have to tell all? Bare all? Leave yourself open to criticism? Yes. Right. Secrecy has no place in research. You have power to shape the story that comes from qualitative material (in contrast to numbers, which speak for themselves more easily), so you have the potential for being "untruthful," for letting *your* biases get in the way of accuracy, even if inadvertently.

ISSUES TO CONSIDER

1. As you begin, remember your intended *audience,* and develop implications for that audience. If more than one, speak clearly to each one.
2. Consider *transferability.* That is, be clear about where and when your findings do (and might) apply. Use examples to distinguish between the two; don't leave consumers to figure it out alone. The history of research is replete with *mis*interpretation!
3. Complement, but don't reshape, findings by interpretation; use lots of evidence. Provide meaning in context, conveying the *gestalt* of your data; in fact, acknowledging context is a strength of qualitative studies. Keep interpretations contextual (to your sample only). That is, think *confirmability*. Offer many exam-

ples, get reports from primary sources, get feedback sessions if possible, and leave an explicit written audit trail so others can follow your process in their minds' eyes.

4. Present findings as exhaustively as possible. When your coding scheme seems to have captured all aspects of each major issue, it's *saturated,* and when your analysis reflects not only major themes as you see them but variations and contradictions, the picture is complete.

5. Work hard to limit your biases through *active self-reflection.* Consciously think about them; make them explicit; get feedback on interpretations from others. Don't get attached to a certain way of coding or early interpretation; stay open to change as analysis progresses. Keep other biases in mind too, such as those of funding sources, and be sure to identify them in your report.

CARRYING OUT THE ANALYSIS

There are different models of qualitative data analysis, and a few moments in the library or bookstore will help you identify a number of possible sources to learn more about them. Here are the basic steps of the grounded theory method of analysis,* a commonly used model.

In essence, qualitative data analysis consists of:

1. *Intratranscript analysis*: try to make meaning of each transcript (transcript referring to the verbatim notes taken during an interview, for example, or audio or video recording that was typed afterward, or the place on a questionnaire that was left for respondents to offer written comments). What do you think the respondent is saying or trying to say? Note each thing (theme, subject, issue, reference) of apparent importance whenever it comes up again in the transcript (by, for example, circling a phrase or paragraph), and use a label or code to note it in the margin. Look for quotes that provide direct evidence of what

---

*See Glaser, B. G. and Strauss, A. L. (1967). *The Discovery of Grounded Theory: Strategies for Qualitative Research.* New York: Aldine de Gruyter.

you think you're hearing, and seek both positive and negative examples.

> Mrs. Jones often talked about the quality of her early education in public school.

The fact that a reference to something is brought up only once does not mean that it isn't important. Think about the quality of what you're reading, not necessarily its quantity.

2. *Intertranscript analysis:* compare and contrast respondents. How is what they say alike? Different? Be prepared for more back and forth thinking (just like problem formulation) as you try to make meaning of respondents *as a group.* Stay open to the evolution of ideas, themes, meaning, etc. For example:

> All respondents talked about their early education. Some went to public school, some to private school, but they all talked about it as an important factor.

In what terms? That's the question to answer now. Read what they said; think about it; reread it; rethink it. For example:

> They all talked about its impact on their current attitudes toward authority.

Okay, now you're beginning to see a collective story from the group about the relationship between early education and adult reactions to authority.

3. *Develop a story* for your sample that includes all of the major themes you've noticed, that includes divergent cases and negative examples to round it out. The question to answer here is how this particular sample has answered your research question.

MAJOR POINTS TO REMEMBER

- At the heart of qualitative analysis is content analysis.
- Analysis begins with clarity about the words and ends with interpretation.

- The concept of evidence is central to qualitative analysis.
- Qualitative analysis includes a "thick description" of every aspect of the study process.
- Some major issues to consider in qualitative analysis are audience, transferability, confirmability, saturation, completeness, range, divergence, and researcher bias.

EXERCISE

A Touch of Practice

1. Read a chapter in any book that particularly interests you, and then close it and put it away.
2. Take out paper and pencil (or the trusty word processor), and take a few pages to write about that chapter. Who is the author? What is the book about? What is the chapter about? What are the major points it tries to make?
3. Go back to that chapter. Now, for each major point that you identified, find an example in that chapter—phrases, sentences, paragraphs, etc.—"evidence" that your identification of the major points are correct, on target.
4. Compare your notes with the chapter. Did you miss anything of importance? If not, then review your notes again. Those major points . . . should they be left as they are, or should you collapse them into categories (themes/points) at a greater level of abstraction? Should themes of education and parental discipline be collapsed into a broader category called childhood experiences, perhaps? Or would that then make them too broad?

No hard and fast rules. Use whatever makes for best representation of the material and best comprehension by the consumer of your work. Perhaps this is a good moment for a feedback session (returning to the source for confirmation of your own comprehension).

Chapter 19

Quantitative Data Analysis:
Making Sense of Descriptive Statistics

(Yes, You *Can*)

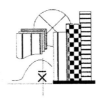

KEY CONCEPTS

description
distribution
frequency
generalization
normal curve
typicality
variation

INTRODUCTION

Descriptive stats are simply numbers that describe your quantitative findings in a visual nutshell through visuals such as tables, charts, and graphs. Commonly associated with large-scale, experimental, and correlational studies, descriptive stats are also found in other studies, if only to give a summary look at certain sample characteristics or demographics, and in many combined-design studies.

COMMON WAYS TO ORGANIZE
DESCRIPTIVE STATS

There are many ways to organize descriptive stats; following are a few common ways.

Frequency Tables

Frequency tables summarize how your sample responded for each variable on your instrument, including sample size, which can vary from item to item according to who did or didn't respond. Sometimes the responses are referred to as "valid" and nonresponses as "missing." Table 19.1 is an example.

Frequency tables often include other basic descriptive stats, such as central tendency (the typical response for that question/item) and variability (how varied the responses are). Keep visuals logical and organized. Table 19.2 organizes values from low (1/no responses) to high (7); at a glance you see that the sample as a whole finds life more rather than less stressful.

You can also describe in detail or in groups. Tables 19.3 and 19.4 illustrate the former and latter approaches, respectively. You decide depending on how much detail you want to offer. For the purpose of your study, do you need to show each actual score, or is grouping enough?

Pie Charts

Pie charts are circular graphs with representative slices that total 100 percent. They're used to depict responses to nominal LOM variables. Figure 19.1 shows religious preference in a sample of 100.

Bar Charts

Bar charts are commonly used to depict responses to ordinal LOM variables. Notice that the bars and spaces between them are of equal width. Figure 19.2 depicts socioeconomic status measured ordinally. In this sample most people below to the low and middle socioeconomic status ranks.

Histograms

Histograms are similar to bar charts but commonly used to show responses to interval or ratio LOM variables. Here, the bars touch to

TABLE 19.1. Example of a Frequency Table

AGE

		Frequency	Percent	Valid Percent	Cumulative Percent
Valid	22	7	7.4	7.5	7.5
	23	11	11.6	11.8	19.4
	24	8	8.4	8.6	28.0
	25	9	9.5	9.7	37.6
	26	10	10.5	10.8	48.4
	27	12	12.6	12.9	61.3
	28	6	6.3	6.5	67.7
	29	3	3.2	3.2	71.0
	30	3	3.2	3.2	74.2
	31	5	5.3	5.4	79.6
	32	1	1.1	1.1	80.6
	33	1	1.1	1.1	81.7
	34	2	2.1	2.2	83.9
	36	2	2.1	2.2	86.0
	37	1	1.1	1.1	87.1
	38	3	3.2	3.2	90.3
	39	2	2.1	2.2	92.5
	42	1	1.1	1.1	93.5
	45	1	1.1	1.1	94.6
	47	1	1.1	1.1	95.7
	49	1	1.1	1.1	96.8
	51	1	1.1	1.1	97.8
	53	2	2.1	2.2	100.0
	Total	93	97.9	100.0	
Missing		2	2.1		
Total		95	100.0		

Note: N = 93; 2 missing; mean age 28.84; median age 27; mode age 27.

show mathematical continuity between the numbers. Figure 19.3 depicts age, a ratio LOM variable. Connecting the tops of each bar by a line renders a kind of curve, and depending on the sample's distribution (how the responses fall), many curve shapes are possible. Figure 19.4 suggests a sample slanted toward the younger age group, revealing a *skewed* distribution.

TABLE 19.2. Example of an Ordinal Low/High Table: How Stressful is Your Job?

		Frequency	Percent	Valid Percent	Cumulative Percent
Not Stressful	2	6	6.9	6.9	6.9
	3	2	2.3	2.3	9.2
	4	8	9.2	9.2	18.4
	5	36	41.4	41.4	59.8
	6	27	31.0	31.0	90.8
Very Stressful	7	8	9.2	9.2	100.0
Total		87	100.0	100.0	100.0

Note: $N = 87$; 0 missing.

TABLE 19.3 Test Scores ($N = 50$)

Score	Frequency	Percent	Cumulative Percent
100	2	4	4
98	3	6	10
97	4	8	18
90	8	16	34
88	12	24	58
85	9	18	76
70	7	14	90
63	4	8	98
51	1	2	100
Total	50	100	100

Contingency Tables (or Crosstabs)

Contingency tables are commonly used to show association between two variables. Table 19.5 depicts association between gender within the sample and their financial status.

Some contingency tables also include percentage figures in each cell under the absolute number.

TABLE 19.4 Test Scores (*N* = 50)

Score	Frequency	Percent	Cumulative Percent
91-100	9	18	18
81-90	29	58	76
71-80	—	—	76
61-70	11	22	98
51-60	1	2	100
Total	50	100	100

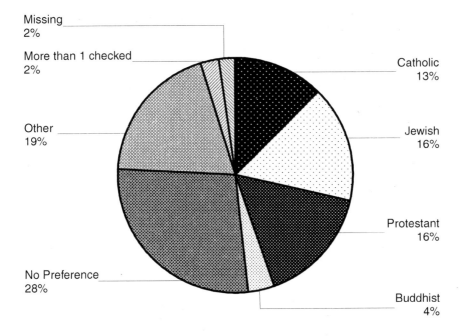

FIGURE 19.1. Example of Pie Chart: Religious Preference (*N* = 100)

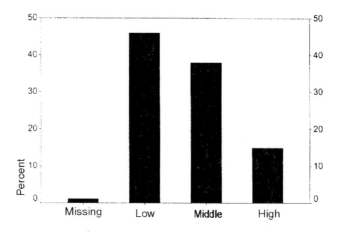

FIGURE 19.2. Example of a Bar Chart: Socioeconomic Status

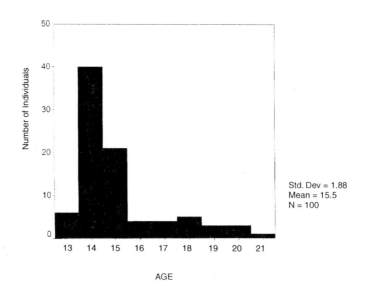

FIGURE 19.3. Example of a Histogram: Age

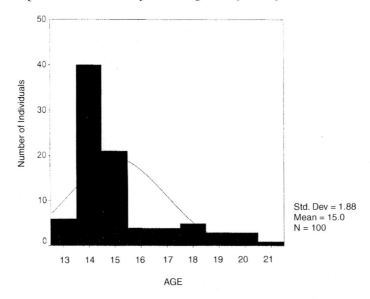

FIGURE 19.4. Example of a Histogram Showing Skewed Distribution of Age

TABLE 19.5. Example of Contingency Table ($N = 86$)

	Financial Status			
Sex	**Overextended**	**Making Ends Meet**	**Comfortable**	**Total**
Male	3	3	1	7
Female	37	30	12	79
Total	40	33	137	86

THREE RULES OF THUMB

1. Always give an overview of the distribution (give it a context so it doesn't just "appear" on the page).
2. Describe each visual to the reader (put into narrative what the figure says graphically).
3. Make an interpretation (what the numbers imply). Be clear.

WHAT ELSE IS DESCRIBED?

Along with the visuals, you usually present *measures of central tendency* (stats that tell what is typical for your sample) on a given variable or the instrument as a whole if it's interval or ratio LOM. Also present *measures of variability* (stats that tell about the nature and size of the variation of individual scores in the sample) on a given variable or the instrument as a whole if it's interval or ratio LOM.

> Central tendency is measured in three different ways: by mode, median, and mean (average).
> Variability is measured in three different ways: index of dispersion, range, and standard deviation.

Think of central tendency as the forest and of variability as the trees; together, they provide a pretty good quantitative picture of your sample.

Measures of Central Tendency

To speak of what's typical about your sample is to speak of *central tendency* (CT). Think about it. Central. Tendency. Each of the three measures of central tendency lends itself to a particular level of measure (LOM/see Chapter 4) and as you'll see, conceptualizes "typicality" in a slightly different way.

Mode

A *mode,* generally used to describe CT for nominal LOM variables, reflects the most often responded category. So if 40 percent of your sample says they are Orthodox, 30 percent Conservative, 20 percent Reform, and 10 percent unaffiliated, the mode for religious affiliation is Orthodox. Note that the mode isn't necessarily a majority of the whole, just the most frequently responded (largest) category. Here, the Orthodox respondents aren't a majority, but their category is still the largest one. The lens used to define CT in this case, then, seeks the largest category. In French the word "mode" means vogue or fashion, so think about which category is in vogue (the one that's most in fashion)—that's the mode.

Median

A *median,* used to describe CT for ordinal, interval, and ratio LOM variables, reflects the middle-most point in your sample's distribution for any given quantitative variable. So, if the distribution for number of years in practice for your sample of twenty social workers falls in the following way:

Sample Member #:   1 2 3 4 5 6 7 8   9 10 11 12 13 14 15 16 17 18 19 20
Years in Practice: 4 4 5 6 7 7 8 9 10 12 13 13 15 17 18 18 19 22 25 26

The median (midpoint) is 12.5 years: half the sample (ten people) have fewer than 12.5 years in practice and half (ten people) have more. Here, then, the lens used to define CT seeks the number above which and below which half the cases fall. Think of the median strip in the highway.

Mean

A *mean* is a mathematical average, and it's best used to describe CT for interval and ratio LOM variables. Based on real math it's considered the most sophisticated CT measure. It's calculated by adding all the numbers or "scores" in a distribution and dividing that sum by the number in that sample. To continue from the previous example, if there are:

twenty members in the sample   = 20
and their sum total number of practice years   = 260
the mean (average) for this sample   = 260 ÷ 20 = 13 (years)

Sometimes the mean represents typicality quite well. Sometimes it doesn't. An extreme score, either high or low, can skew a distribution so much that the mean isn't a good representation; if so, the mode or median are better (more accurate) measures to use.

Measures of Variability

Measures of variability indicate the extent to which individual scores in any distribution (years in practice, ages, height, number of men in caseload, SAT scores, etc.) disperse—or spread out—around their mean. Say the mean score on a test taken by twenty-five people is eighty. You know the "average" score for this distribution, but you don't know how widely individual scores vary around that mean. By knowing variability, you get a fuller picture.

Index of Dispersion

Index of dispersion shows variability for nominal LOM variables by reflecting the percentage of cases that fall outside the mode. If the mode is a category with 35 percent of the scores in it, the index of dispersion is .65. In this example, there's quite a bit of variation, because 65 percent of the sample is not reflected by the mode.

Range

The *range* shows variability for ordinal, interval, and ratio LOM variables and refers to the size of spread between a distribution's highest and lowest numbers. What's the lowest test score (or years in practice or age or weight) for your sample? And what's the highest? The difference between the two is the range (r).

Standard Deviation

The *standard deviation* (SD) stat (number) shows variability for interval and ratio LOM variables and is calculated from the mean. It speaks to average distance of the individual scores from the mean. The greater that variability, the larger the SD stat.

Calculated how? Basically, probability theory says that in every naturally occurring phenomenon, a few cases always have much less of whatever attribute is being measured, a few always have much more of it, and that most cases cluster around the average (mean).

Think about your school tests. Don't a few people always do very poorly, a few always do really well, and most do somewhere in the middle? That's a real-life example of this theory, which, in action, is called the *normal curve*. A visual rendition of this mathematical concept is shown in Figure 19.5.

Probability theory says that in any *normal* distribution (not too skewed by high or low scores):

1. about 68 percent of the scores will always fall within a specific distance to either side (+/–) of the mean, that distance on each side called one standard deviation;

2. about 95 percent of the scores will always fall within a specific distance to either side (+/–) of the mean, that distance on each side called two standard deviations; and
3. over 99 percent of the scores will always fall within a specific distance to either side (+/–) of the mean, that distance on each side called three standard deviations (making a total of six).

So, picture yourself standing on the top center of the normal curve depicted in Figure 19.5. This puts you where the mean, median, and mode meet. Now look as far as one SD to each side; you should see about 68 percent of everyone's score. Now look as far as two SD to each side; you should see about 95 percent of them. Now look as far as three SD to each side; you should see over 99 percent of them.

Translated into the real world, say a classroom of twenty-five students takes a test with a resulting mean score of 80 and an SD value of 5. For this distribution, each standard deviation unit is five points:

+1 SD includes all scores as far up as 85
–1 SD includes all scores as far down as 75
+2 SD includes all scores as far up as 90
–2 SD includes all scores as far down as 70
+3 SD includes all scores as far up as 95
–3 SD includes all scores as far down as 65

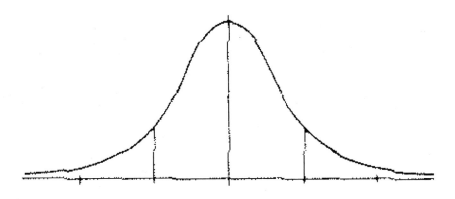

FIGURE 19.5. Example of Normal Curve

Now, if you were to get on top of the mean for this particular distribution, which would put you at the number 80,

1. 5 test-score points to either side of you (85-75 or +/–1 SD) would include about 68 percent of the class scores.
2. 10 test-score points to either side (90-70 or +/–2 SD) would include about 95 percent of the class scores.
3. 15 test-score points to either side (95-65 or +/–3 SD) would include just about all the scores.

In this sample there's quite a bit of variation. However, if the mean were 80 with an SD value of 2

1. you'd find about 68 percent of the scores between 82 and 78 (+/–1 SD);
2. you'd find about 95 percent of them between 84 and 76 (+/–2 SD); and
3. you'd find over 99 percent of them between 86 and 74 (+/–3 SD)

Now the individual scores hover more closely to one another around the mean indicating that members scored pretty closely to one another and thus reflecting less variability.

Why Should You Care?

For one thing, as noted previously, it's useful to know just how well the mean actually represents the sample. The larger the standard deviation value, the greater the variability, meaning that individual scores tend to *dis*resemble the average.

Second, it provides a language for comparing numbers when they're used differently. Say you give a group of people two tests: a self-esteem measure that scores from 70-100 and an eating-habits test that scores from 1-10. Group A's mean score is 85 on the self-esteem test and 6 on the eating-habits test. How can you compare their scores? You can't. Say Mrs. Smith scored an 85 on the self-esteem test and a 7 on the eating-habits test. How can you compare 85 and 7? You can't. The numbers are used so differently that it's the old apples and oranges problem. However, it's in this very kind of comparison that social work is often interested. What to do?

We translate the values (actual scores) into standard deviation units, which reflect variation (deviation) from the mean (from any mean), and voila! We have a language (referred to as *z* scores) that provides a common denominator for comparing apples and oranges.

MAJOR POINTS TO REMEMBER

- Statistics are numbers.
- Descriptive stats summarize your quantitative findings and are often presented in visual nutshells through tables, charts, and graphs.
- Three measures of central tendency describe what's typical for your sample: mode, median, and mean.
- Three measures of variability describe variation within your sample: index of dispersion, range, and standard deviation.

EXERCISE

1. Match the description to the visual:
   - _____ circular graph   a. Bar chart
   - _____ bars touch one another   b. Histogram
   - _____ bars do not touch one another   c. Pie chart
2. Match the description to the visual:
   - _____ commonly used to depict
     nominal LOM variables   a. Bar chart
   - _____ commonly used to depict
     ordinal LOM variables   b. Histogram
   - _____ commonly used to depict
     interval/ratio LOM variables   c. Pie chart
3. You have ordinal LOM data. The mean will be a good measure of central tendency. True/False
4. You have interval LOM data. Index of dispersion will be a good measure of central tendency. True/False
5. The mode reflects the middle-most point in a distribution. True/False

6. You have nominal LOM data. The median will be a good measure of variability. True/False
7. Index of dispersion is a good measure of typicality. True/False
8. You have interval LOM data. The range is a possible measure of variability. True/False
9. The larger the variation of individual scores in a distribution, the larger the SD stat. True/False
10. The mean, median, and mode of a normal curve always coincide. True/False

---

Answers: (1) C, B, A; (2) C, A, B; (3) False (mode); (4) False (index of dispersion is a measure of variability); (5) False (median); (6) False (index of dispersion); (7) False (a measure of variability); (8) True; (9) True; (10) True.

Chapter 20

Quantitative Data Analysis: Making Sense of Inferential Statistics

(Yes, You *Can . . . Really!*)

KEY CONCEPTS

association
confidence
correlation
difference
directionality
inference
probability
sample error
statistical power
statistical significance

INTRODUCTION

Inferential stats tell you:

1. if difference or association is significant (real/true/accurate) within your sample or probably due to chance or some error in sampling; and

2. if you can infer that the look (characteristics) of the population resembles the look (characteristics) of the sample and, as a result, with what level of confidence you can generalize from your sample to its population.

Remember we're talking here about *quantitative* data (inherently numerical or numerically coded in some way) in *probability* samples.

HOW TO USE INFERENTIAL STATISTICS

To use inferential stats means to carry out certain mathematical computations (now done by computer programs such as *SPSS*) called *tests of statistical significance*. There are many such tests. They're all based on your descriptive stats, but different tests are used in different ways using different mathematical calculations. The one you use depends on the LOM of the variable(s) in question. Again, they all answer these questions:

1. Can I infer that a difference or association noted in this sample is significant, or is it probably just a chance thing or due to sampling error?
2. Can I infer that the look of my population resembles the look of my sample enough to confidently generalize whatever I find of significance for one (sample) to the other (population)?

Say you give a standardized test on verbal skills to two randomly assigned groups of children. Experimental group scores range from 50 to 75, mean = 60. Control group scores: range from 52 to 76, mean = 60. You have a few descriptive stats for each group: (1) lowest/highest scores, (2) range, (3) and mean.

You now give a skills program to the experimental group and you give a skills book to all members of a comparison group to read on their own. The program ends, and you give everyone the test again. Experimental group posttest scores range from 55 (+5 pts) to 85 (+10), mean = 70 (+10). Okay! Things look up for your program! Control group posttest scores range from 55 (+3 pts) to 82 (+ 6), mean = 65 (+5). Huh! They did better too! *Huh?*

Here's the thing. There *seems* to be a difference between the two groups at posttest. Your experimental group had higher scores at the end of your program, but so did the control group (not an unrealistic scenario).

Now what? How do you know if the difference between them is significant (far away enough from what chance would have dictated anyway)—that the experimental group did better *as a result of* your program? You don't, but if you subject your descriptive stats to significance testing, you can find out.

Using probability theory and calculating mathematical relationships between descriptive stats, significance tests let you infer whether a difference (or correlation) is *significant* (greater than that which chance alone would have dictated) and, if so, with just what level of confidence you can generalize that difference or correlation to the sample's population—just how likely what you find in your sample "holds water" for its parent population.

Since inference by any other name always denotes uncertainty, probability theory is integral to inferential stats. Basically, probability theory says that more likely than not what you find is not significant; and the job of inferential stats is to evaluate the odds of making a mistake if you do claim significance.

THREE RELATED LAWS OF PROBABILITY

Three important laws of probability (paraphrased here) guide the calculation of inferential stats:

1. No matter how good your random sampling strategy, even if a stat test suggests that a finding is significant (real/true/accurate), you still must acknowledge at least one chance of being incorrect due to an unknown but possible bias in your sample *(sample error).*

This "humanity factor" is acknowledged as *margin of error* (or minimum sample error) and is calculated from standard deviation units (now called *standard error units;* same thing different name). Clearly, the smaller it is the better. Practically speaking, your random sample better be truly random. Cheating makes all your findings meaningless!

2. Don't worry that random sampling ten times in one population gets you ten different samples because over the long run (many samples), as long as those samples have integrity (are truly random), their distributions tend to look very similar. This law is called the *Central Limit Theorem* (CLT).

Thus, no matter which of many possible samples from a population you end up with, if it's truly random you can have a 95 percent confidence level (95 percent probability) that the average population score for any distribution will be within +/− 2 standard error units of your sample's average score.

Remember standing on top of the normal curve at its mean and looking to either side as far as 1 SD, 2 SD, and 3 SD to see how individual scores varied from their average? Get back up there. Now look only as far as *two* of those units to either side. The CLT says that whatever the mean is for your sample (unless it has only thirty or fewer members or is badly skewed), you have a 95 percent chance that somewhere within that four-unit space is the average score for your population.

Why care? Because this 95 percent confidence level has been established in social science as the minimum level for claiming significance of any kind and is factored into the math of all stat tests. So, you can only claim significance and generalizability if the test says you have a 95 percent or better chance of being correct (indicated by the *p* level at the end of every test). If it says you have a 94 percent chance (*p*. 06) of being correct, forget about claims of significance or generalizability. If it says that you have a 95 percent (*p*. 05) chance of being correct, clap your hands; and if it says that you have a 98 percent (*p*. 02) chance of being correct, jump for joy!

3. The larger your sample the more likely its mean will resemble that of its population. This is called the *Law of Large Numbers*.

A random sample of fifty has more chances to resemble its population of 100 than a random sample of ten. So the larger the sample the better if your aim is to generalize from sample population to the other.

THE TESTING PROCESS

All inferential stats are based on testing either a hypothesis of group difference or a hypothesis of association (correlation), each of which can be formulated at a broad level:

> There's a significant difference in how Group A and Group B scored overall on this instrument, or
> There's a significant association between the overall scores on Measure A (one instrument) and Measure B (another instrument) for this one group.

At a more detailed level:

> There's a significant difference in how Group A and Group B scored on Item #5, or
> There's a significant association between the overall scores on Item #4 (one variable) and Item #6 (another variable) for this one group.

Hypothesis of Group Difference

This compares 2 or more groups on one variable:

You wonder: Is there a significant difference between Group A and Group B on this variable?

You hypothesize: There is a significant difference between the groups.

And then you formulate a null version:

No siree, there's *no* significant difference between the groups.

You subject the null version to a stat test and check results. If the test says to reject it with a 95 percent confidence level (yes!) you can substantiate the original hypothesis.

The two types of groups for which we test difference are as follows:

1. *independent sample groups* (most random samples), and
2. *correlated sample groups* (*longitudinal samples* in which your preintervention and postintervention samples are conceptualized as two different groups [even with the same members], and *matching groups* in which some members are in the sample only because of their relationship to other members [husbands of wives, siblings of siblings, clients of workers, etc.]).

The groups must be distinguished because the stat tests for each type use slightly different math. Independent-group testing is usually interested in raw scores as well as comparison, and correlated-group testing is primarily interested in comparison (e.g., how husbands and wives compare on a marital satisfaction test) and so seeks fewer stats.

Hypothesis of Association

This examines association in one group on 2 or more variables:

You wonder: Is there a significant correlation between age and income for this sample?

You hypothesize: There is a significant correlation between age and income for this sample.

And then you formulate a null version:

No siree, there's *no* significant correlation between age and income in this sample.

You subject the null version to a stat test and check results. If the test says to reject it with a 95 percent confidence level (yes!) you can substantiate your original hypothesis.

DIRECTIONALITY

Whether you want to test difference or association, the hypothesis can be stated in either *directional* or *nondirectional* terms.

Directional hypothesis of group   Girls exercise longer each week difference: than do boys.

Nondirectional hypothesis:	There's a significant difference between girls and boys in amount of weekly exercise.
Directional hypothesis of association:	Attitude increases income.
Nondirectional hypothesis:	Attitude and income are associated.

A directional version predicts the nature of difference (girls do more) or association (attitude has an impact on income, not vice versa), whereas a nondirectional version proposes a difference or association without predicting its nature.

If you think you're "intelligent" enough to predict the nature of a difference or association, go ahead and formulate a directional version. If, however, the stat reveals the opposite of what you predicted, too bad! You must refute your hypothesis. If you want to play it safe by not predicting nature, formulate a nondirectional version. Then, whatever difference or association the test reveals, you can substantiate your hypothesis.

IN A NUTSHELL

To test statistical significance of any quantitative finding:

1. Transform your question of interest into a hypothesis of group difference or association, either directional or nondirectional. (How bold you are?)
2. Transform that hypothesis into its null version.
3. Subject that null hypothesis to a stat test.
4. If and *only* if that test rejects your null hypothesis with a 95 percent or higher confidence level, accept your original hypothesis.

SIGNIFICANCE TESTING: POSSIBILITIES FOR ERROR

The math involved in stat testing has been developed and refined over a long period of time and with great care. However, these tests still might make two types of errors:

1. An *alpha* error (Type A/Type One): the test says it's okay to accept your hypothesis (reject the null) when really, if the truth

were known, you should refute it. Uh oh! Here you go, claiming significance or association when there really isn't any.

2. A *beta* error (Type B/Type Two): the test tells you to reject your hypothesis (accept the null) when really, if the truth were known, you should accept it. Oh, dear! Here you go, crying over no significance or association when really there is one!

How to prevent such catastrophe?

1. Integrity of sampling method is essential—so don't cheat. Also, say your final sample is only eighty questionnaires out of 150 sent out. That's a pretty big difference. How do you know some special bias hasn't crept into that final sample? Pay attention to these possibilities up front.

2. Using the right stat test for the right variable LOM is important; the incorrect one can yield incorrect results.

   How mathematically sensitive a test is to reduce the potential for making either one of these two possible errors is referred to as its *statistical power.* The group of tests (called *parametric* tests) that examine difference/association at the interval/ratio LOM are much more powerful than those (*nonparametric* tests) that examine difference/association at the nominal/ordinal LOM because they use numbers in a real way (unlike numbers used to code ordinal data, for example).

   The more powerful tests are based on certain assumptions about the sample and should be used only when those assumptions are met in reality. Because they've shown themselves to be such good indicators of significance even when the assumptions are not fully met, however, they often get used at the nominal/ordinal LOM as well. They shouldn't.

How to know the probability of making these errors? Look for the *p* value at the end of every stat test. It tells you the probability that an alpha or beta error will be have been made if you substantiate your hypothesis. Thus, *p.* 04 means if you claim significance you have four chances in 100 (4 percent) according to that test of being incorrect (making an alpha or beta error); *p.* 11 says you have 11 chances in

100 (11 percent) of being incorrect. And *p*. 001 says you have one chance in a thousand of being incorrect.

One chance in a thousand of being incorrect . . . that seems acceptable. Four chances in 100? Not too bad. Eleven in 100? Now *that's* scary! Would you be willing to make the following claim, say, in all the newspapers of the world?

> According to my research, there's a significant difference in intelligence between the genders. . . . The statistical testing process indicates that I have 11 chances in 100 of being wrong on this, but I'm willing to accept those odds.

What do you think? Could you take that risk? Social science won't. The social science research convention is to claim significance only if *p* (probability of being mistaken) is .05 or smaller. Basically, it says this: If the test says I have five chances or fewer in 100 of being mistaken in claiming significance, that's not bad; I can live with those odds.

So for social science research *p*. 05 is acceptable. But that's the limit. *P* .06 is not acceptable. And no, it's not *almost* acceptable. Of course, different sciences have different conventions, and even within them the conventions vary according to the consequences of being mistaken. For example, *p*. 01, which is excellent for social science, may not be acceptable to medical research, which often requires a much greater confidence level, such as *p* .001—one chance in 1,000 of making a mistake in making claims around the likelihood of a new drug's causing birth defects, for example.

STATISTICAL SIGNIFICANCE VERSUS MEANING

Statistical significance and meaning: How do they relate to each other? Remember that statistical significance is the result of a mathematical calculation that indicates the probability of a difference or association between quantitative findings being a real/true/accurate representation or just a chance thing or due to some error in your research process:

Yes, the difference/association you're testing is probably real/true/ accurate, and here are the odds that you'll be mistaken if you say so.

No, the difference/association you're testing is probably not real/true/accurate.

Yes, what you see and find in your sample probably also holds true for its parent population.

No, what you see and find in your sample probably doesn't hold true for its population.

Now you need to make meaning of the results. What does significance or lack thereof suggest given the purpose of your study? What can be learned from the results within the context of your study? What questions can be answered? What new ones can be raised? You've described your findings; now interpret them within the context of your study and then in context of your research topic and what others have found. That's how you make meaning of your stats and use them to add to the existing body of knowledge.

Significance testing is a means to an end, then, not an end in and of itself. It is useful toward intra-sample meaning of quantitative data (what you can infer from the results for the sample itself) and extra-sample meaning (what you can infer to and thus know about the population of interest). Only when statistical significance is considered, analyzed, and presented in real-world terms does it take on *meaning*.

MAJOR POINTS TO REMEMBER

- Inferential stats are numbers that tell you if your findings are significant for your sample and how confidently you can generalize them to the population.
- Inferential stats are based on descriptive stats.
- To produce inferential stats is to carry out tests of statistical significance.
- Statistical significance tests use different descriptive stats and different mathematics, depending on the LOM of the variable(s) to be tested.

- Inferential stats are guided by three laws of probability regarding (1) potential for sample error, (2) resemblance of random samples in a population, and (3) sample size.
- Tests of statistical significance test hypotheses of group difference or of association.
- Each type of hypothesis has directional and nondirectional versions, each of which has its own particular test version.
- Two types of errors can be made in testing inference: alpha, when a test rejects a null hypothesis by mistake, and beta, when it accepts a null hypothesis by mistake.
- Integrity of sample and using appropriate tests can help to prevent such errors.
- The mathematical sensitivity of a test to reduce the potential for making either error is referred to as its statistical power.
- *P* levels indicate the probability of making such errors if significance is claimed.
- The social science research convention is to accept significance at *p*. 05 or higher confidence level.

EXERCISE

Test Yourself

1. You only need to use statistical significance tests if you can't tell significance from eyeballing the data. True/False
2. Inferential stats apply only to experimental and correlational designs. True/False
3. A 95 percent confidence level means that if a test indicates significant difference or association and you make that claim, you have five chances in 100 of being incorrect. True/False
4. Directionality applies only to hypotheses of group difference. True/False
5. *P*. 04 means you have six chances in 100 of making an incorrect claim of significance about your hypothesis. True/False
6. Inferential stats help you determine the degree to which you can safely generalize from a sample to a population. True/False

7. Size of sample doesn't matter when working with inferential stats as long as you used some kind of random-sampling method to obtain it. True/False
8. Statistical power refers to the credibility of your quantitative data. True/False
9. You've carried out your study. Through friends and acquaintances you've found thirty people to interview, and you've transcribed and numerically coded their narratives. Which of these inferential processes can you use?
   - You can develop a hypothesis of difference based on what you've learned about your sample, and subject it to testing for significance.
   - You can develop a hypothesis of association based on what you've learned about your sample, and subject it to testing for significance.
   - You can use the codes to calculate central tendency and subject those stats to inference testing.

Answers: (1) False; (2) False; (3) True; (4) False (it applies to hypotheses of association as well); (5) False (4 chances out of 100); (6) True; (7) False; (8) False; (9) None! (no random sampling involved, and qualitative data codes aren't used as a basis for descriptive or inferential stats).

Chapter 21

Tests of Statistical Significance

(Gaining *Confidence!*)

KEY CONCEPTS

association
confidence level
correlated samples
correlation coefficient
critical value
group difference
independent samples
level of measure
one-tailed test
probability
statistical significance
test value
two-tailed test

INTRODUCTION

All statistical significance tests yield a statistic (number); a t test yields a t stat, an F test an F stat, a chi-square test a chi-square stat, etc. That stat is referred to as the test *value,* and with the exception of one type of test, it can range from 1 to 3, based on the three standard error units (known by descriptive stats as standard deviation units) to either side of a distributions's mean score.

Probability theory (always thumbing its nose!) says that our chances of finding significant difference or association are zero (nil, none, nada). So, the farther away from zero the test value, the more likely that any significance noted by the test's math is real/true/accurate. Although a test value (except for one type of test) might range from 1 to 3, the point at which it begins to reflect significance, known as its *critical value,* is 1.96. So a test value must be 1.96 or greater for you to claim that a difference or association noted by that test is, in fact, significant. In this case, then, bigger is better!

CHOOSING A TEST

This is how you select the correct test:

1. You choose to enter one of two "families" of tests: the one that tests *significance of group difference* or the one that tests *significance of association* (correlation). Remember these from the previous chapter?
2. You then select the test that's correct for the level at which the variable(s) in question have been measured (nominal, ordinal, interval, or ratio LOM). For tests of group difference, you select tests that are appropriate for testing independent sample groups or correlated sample groups.
3. You then go to the directional or nondirectional version of that test, depending on how you formulated your hypothesis to be tested.
   - The directional version, called *one tailed,* looks only in the distribution's (curve's) tails that can confirm or refute the direction of your hypothesis; it doesn't tell you if the opposite of your hypothesis is true, for example.
   - The nondirectional version, called *two tailed,* is a kinder, gentler version. Not as picky as its directional counterpart, it looks throughout the distribution (curve) for any difference or association whatsoever (a nondirectional hypothesis is willing to take any difference or association it can find, remember?).

4. You subject your descriptive stats to testing as called for by that particular test, and you examine the results primarily for two things: (1) the test stat (value) and (2) the confidence *(p)* level.

COMMON TESTS OF GROUP DIFFERENCE

Chi-Square

Chi-square generally tests independent sample difference between 2 or more groups, (1) on nominal LOM data or (2) when distribution is very skewed. Chi-square is a very common test in social work research because so much data of interest is measured at the nominal LOM.

The test calculates the difference between your findings (observed frequency) and what probability would normally dictate (expected frequency). If the chi-square stat (value) is significant at the p. 05 or higher confidence level, you can substantiate your hypothesis that a significant difference exists between the groups. Calculated on the actual number of cases in the groups rather than means, a chi-square stat (value) is always much larger than those of other tests.

Fisher Exact is used instead for two groups of small independent samples (thirty or fewer). *McNemar Change* and *Cochran Q* examine correlated sample difference between two and two or more groups, respectively, on nominal LOM data.

Mann-Whitney U

Mann-Whitney U tests independent sample difference between two groups on ordinal LOM data. Since numbers have no inherent value here except as codes, the test ranks the members of each group and then compares either their actual or averaged ranks. If the U stat (value) is 1.96 or larger at a p. 05 or higher confidence level, you can substantiate your hypothesis that a significant difference exists between the groups.

Kruskal-Wallis tests independent-sample difference between two or more groups. *Wilcoxon t* and *Friedman ANOVA* (analysis of variance) test correlated sample difference between two and two or more groups, respectively, on ordinal LOM data.

·*t Test*

An *independent t* test examines independent sample difference between two groups on interval or ratio LOM data by comparing the difference in their means. If the *t* stat (value) is 1.96 or larger at a *p*. 05 or higher confidence level, you can substantiate your hypothesis that exists a significant difference between the groups.

Say you give a scholastic aptitude test to two groups. You then calculate the mean of each. Group A has a mean of 800; Group B has a mean of 750. Is that a significant difference between them? We don't know, but through certain math calculations based on their means and variance, a *t test* tells you if it probably is or isn't. If the test says it is, then it is. Difference cannot be a little or kind of or almost significant. It is, or it isn't.

ANOVA (aka *F test*) examines *independent sample difference* between two or more groups. *Correlated t* and *correlated samples F test* examine correlated sample difference between two and two or more groups, respectively, on interval or ratio LOM.

COMMON TESTS OF ASSOCIATION

To examine *correlation* is to look at the nature of a relationship between variables (not cause and effect, but if they have a meaningful relationship), such as possible association between culture and attitude or incarceration and recidivism or personal history and present behavior or gender and experience, etc. Just as tests of difference are based on variables' LOM, so are tests of association.

Phi Coefficient

Phi coefficient tests association when each variable has only two categories (such as variable one with *male/female* response options and variable two with *yes/no* response options).

Contingency Coefficient

Contingency coefficient tests association when the variables have equal but more than two categories (such as variable one with three response options of *Muslim/Jewish/Christian* and variable two with response options of *under 30/30 to 50/over 50* years old).

Spearman's Rho

Spearman's rho tests association between ordinal LOM variables by comparing ranks on each variable. Although *Spearman's rho* is the technically correct test to use, *Pearson's r,* intended to measure association for interval/ratio LOM variables, has been proven to be so good at measuring ordinal LOM data as well that it's often used instead. *Spearman's rho* is also used when assumptions necessary for *Pearson's r* (the more powerful test) cannot be met and the researcher is paying attention to that fact!

Pearson's r

Pearson's r tests association between interval or ratio LOM variables by comparing means on each variable and yields an *r* stat (value), commonly referred to as a *correlation coefficient.* When you want to examine association between two variables that have different LOM's, use whichever test is appropriate for the variable with the lower LOM.

Talking About Correlation

A *correlation coefficient* (cc) can range from weak to strong (within a range of 0 to 1) and be either positive (+) or negative (–). Thus, a correlation might be weak or moderate or strong in either positive or negative territory.

A *positive correlation* is when the variables covary in the same direction ("more" of one variable, whatever it reflects, with "more" of the other, whatever it reflects). Higher self-esteem with higher education? Positive correlation. Lower self-esteem with lower education? Positive correlation.

A *negative correlation* is when the variables covary in opposite directions ("more" of one variable, whatever it reflects, with "less" of the other, whatever it reflects). Higher incidence of attention-seeking behaviors with lower self-esteem? Negative correlation.

Here's the scale for assessing strength and direction:*

−1.00	=	perfect negative correlation
− .95	=	strong negative correlation
− .50	=	moderate negative correlation
− .10	=	weak negative correlation
− .00	=	no correlation at all
+ .10	=	weak positive correlation
+ .50	=	moderate positive correlation
+ .95	=	strong positive correlation
+1.00	=	perfect positive correlation (e.g., something correlated with itself)

Here too, however, note the p level at the end of the test, which must be p. 05 or higher to substantiate your hypothesis of association.

DEGREES OF FREEDOM

Most stat tests factor into their calculations the amount of variation that must occur around the mean (or ranks or actual cell count) of each group being compared before their difference is probably *not* significant. A *degrees of freedom* (df) stat is generally presented as a real number (1, 2, 6, etc.) and, usually, the larger the sample the smaller it is. Degrees of freedom are calculated from either (1) the number of groups being compared or (2) the number of people (cases) in each sample or (3) both.

MULTIVARIATE ANALYSIS

Multivariate testing refers to tests that examine several groups around several variables and several variables around several groups. There are many of them, they're quite complex, and with them, you begin to move into advanced stats.

---

*For nominal LOM variables directionality doesn't apply, just strength; so signs don't apply.

MAJOR POINTS TO REMEMBER

- All statistical significance tests yield a statistic, referred to as a test *value*.
- The larger the test value, the more likely that any significance noted by the test's math is real/true/accurate.
- Selecting a proper test includes choosing one of difference or association; one that's appropriate to the data's LOM (and for tests of difference, one appropriate to either independent or cor-related sample groups); and either a one-tailed or two-tailed test version, depending on the nature of hypothesis.
- A few common tests of group difference are chi-square, Fisher Exact, McNemar Change, Cochran Q for nominal LOM data; Mann-Whitney U, Kruskal-Wallis, Wilcoxon t, and Friedman ANOVA for ordinal LOM data; and independent t, ANOVA/F test, correlated t, and correlated samples F test for interval and ratio LOM data.
- A few common tests of association are phi coefficient, contin-gency coefficient, Spearman's rho, and Pearson's r.
- To examine association between two variables of different LOM use the test appropriate to the lower LOM.
- Correlation coefficients (cc), the stats that result from associa-tion testing, range from weak to strong (from 0 to 1) and can be positive or negative.
- Degrees of freedom (df) speak to the amount of variation that can occur in each distribution being compared before a differ-ence or association is determined as probably not significant. A df stat is factored into the calculations of most tests.
- Degrees of freedom are calculated from either the number of groups being compared or number of people (cases) in each sample or both.

EXERCISE

Test Yourself

1. For all but one statistical significance test, the test stat (value) can range from:
   a. 1 to 3
   b. 1 to 4
   c. 2 to 3

2. The closer to zero the test stat (value), the more probable that any significance noted by the test's math is real/true/accurate. True/False
3. The critical value of most tests is:
   a. 1.00
   b. 1.96
   c. 2.96
4. A positive correlation coefficient is said to be strong, and a negative one is said to be weak. True/False
5. +1.00 and −1.00 are both perfect correlations. True/False
6. Match the test to the data to be tested: A. chi-square; B. Contingency; C. Mann-Whitney U; D. Pearson's r; E. Phi; F. Spearman's Rho; G. t test

   _____ group difference for nominal LOM data
   _____ group difference for ordinal LOM data
   _____ group difference for interval/ratio LOM data
   _____ association between nominal LOM variables with two categories each
   _____ association between nominal LOM variables with three or more but equal number categories each
   _____ association between ordinal LOM variables
   _____ association between interval or ratio LOM variables

7. You decide to carry out a longitudinal study of the impact of a special group program for teenagers on conflict resolution skills. You are able to random select a sample of twenty to participate in your group, which will take place once a week for ten weeks. Before the program begins, you give each sample member a Conflict Resolution Skills Test to assess current skill level. You carry out your program, test them again with the same instrument, and test them again every six months for the next two years. These two groups are:
   _____ independent samples
   _____ correlated samples
   Why? _____
   _____

8. You then decide to see if at the last posttest there are any differences between the males and females in the sample around overall skill level as measured by the test. You are testing a hypothesis of:

_____group difference

_____association

Why?_____

---

9. You decide that girls probably have a higher skill level than boys. Therefore you formulate your hypothesis as:

_____directional

_____nondirectional

Why?_____

---

10. The test of statistical significance you then subject your hypothesis to is a:

_____one-tailed version

_____two-tailed version

Why?_____

---

*Answers: (1) a; (2) False; (3) b.; (4) False; (5) True; (6) A, C, G, E, B, F, D; (7) Correlated samples; (8) Association (you're testing in one sample association between two variables: gender and skill level); (9) Directional hypothesis; (10) One-tailed version.

Chapter 22

Wrapping It Up
(Endnote)

At the beginning of this book I said my hope is that this will help you, the reader, make both intellectual and practical sense of research methods for social work. Now, at the end, I want to reiterate that this book is intended as an *adjunct* resource to a textbook, not as a replacement, and that much of the decision making called for in research needs to take place with those in the know—researchers, theoreticians, scholars, practitioners, or consumers.

I hope that reading this material has enhanced your ability to pick out the essence of the methods—what *must* be done, either conceptually or practically, before anything else can or should be done. I also hope that it has given you a sense of the kind of play that goes on in the process as well—play in terms of kicking around ideas and play in terms of the back-and-forth dancing that often takes place in order to move ahead.

More specifically, I said that I hoped this book would help you feel more confident about engaging in research. I hope that it has anticipated some of your major (and perhaps unexpressed) concerns, answered some of your major questions, given you a better understanding of where you and your ideas fit into the world of possibilities, and, in so doing, helped you to be less daunted by the formidable reputation that research has assumed over the years and to be open to meeting the challenge in a way that has professional meaning for you.

Chapter 1 attempted to help you find the right question to ask (you know the old joke, *I've got the answer, now who's got the question?*), acknowledging this process of problem formulation as probably the most challenging step as you confront the endless possibilities. Chapter 2 attempted to anchor that process in the real world in general and the real world of social work, more specifically, by discussing the interplay between what others have studied in your area of interest and formulating a useful and realistic question. Chapter 3 attempted to help you understand the difference between hypothesis-driven and question-driven research. Chapter 4 gave you an overview of the role and use of variables and demanded some specificity from your thinking. Chapter 5 warned you to examine your assumptions lest they make an ass out of u and me. Chapter 6 provided an overview of design types and, I hope, clarified the connection between purpose and design.

In describing the highlights of each of the design types, along with an outline of methods and examples, Chapters 7 through 13 tried to give you a sense of how various designs might (or might not) fit your current interest. Chapter 14 took a brief look at instrument design with particular attention to developing measures that are reliable and valid. Chapter 15 described methods and implications of selecting samples, and Chapter 16 outlined the major advantages and disadvantages of data-collection methods.

As an opening to analysis, Chapter 17 offered an overview of each method, and Chapter 18 offered a look at the major concepts and steps of qualitative data analysis. Chapters 19 through 21 provided a look at the major concepts and steps of quantitative data analysis. Hopefully, they did so without causing you to tremble.

Of course, the research process does not end with analysis. Analysis is a springboard, really, to the development of further research. Yes, of course, it answers your research question, but if you look carefully, it probably raises as many if not more questions than it answers! That's the fun of it! We never, ever run out of questions. We're fated to keep asking, but each time we do so, we ask slightly more sophisticated questions. Just as a realistic goal in practice is to make increasingly sophisticated rather than no mistakes at all, so goes the questioning process of research. Always more to ask, more to know, more to ask—but each time with a little more knowledge. What's most important is that what gets asked and answered be applied—that is, that the process helps us do whatever it is that we do, better even as we ask yet more questions.

Index